D1280216

The World of Graft

THE
WORLD *of* GRAFT

By

JOSIAH FLYNT

 BOOKS FOR LIBRARIES PRESS
FREEPORT, NEW YORK

First Published 1901
Reprinted 1971

INTERNATIONAL STANDARD BOOK NUMBER:
0-8369-5694-X

LIBRARY OF CONGRESS CATALOG CARD NUMBER:
72-150181

PRINTED IN THE UNITED STATES OF AMERICA

To Those Who Have
" Squared It "

Contents

PART I

INTRODUCTORY

THE WORLD OF GRAFT

Introductory

MUNICIPAL government in the United States has been criticised heretofore almost exclusively from the reformer's point of view. The great majority of the books, pamphlets, and magazine articles dealing with this subject have come from the pens of Upper World critics. The man who makes his living off the maladministration of our large cities has never been really heard. As a reformer, he says, in a different idiom, more or less what the social scientist says; as a professional thief, or tramp, still actively engaged in his business, he has not been persuaded to say anything of importance. Neither of the two " committees " which have recently investigated New York City was successful in getting him to " open up "; and the only books of value he has ever written in this country were written after he had decided to " square it " and live respectably. He is not a garrulous person; he must know absolutely with whom he is talking before he will enter into an intimate conversation.

The present book is the outcome of a mod-

The World of Graft

erately successful effort to convince him that he was talking to a " pal." In some cases he knew that he was to be quoted, but in all cases he was convinced before talking that what he said would not be hurled back upon him by any of the Powers that Rule. Occasionally he talked because he was " sore "—some of the Powers that Rule had treated him unfairly, and he wanted to " roast " them—and then again, merely to satisfy the curiosity of an old acquaintance. My purpose in trying to get him to talk was to hear the Under World's criticism of the Upper World's system of municipal defence against crime. In every large city in the United States these two worlds rub up against each other; the professional thief goes up-town to live when he has made his " pile " or is temporarily in luck, just as surely as the aristocrat goes down-town when his " pile " has been exhausted. Sociologically the thief is invariably classified as a down-town resident; the scientists seem unable to consider him seriously outside of the realm of theory. While the scientists are talking and writing about him, however, he is comfortably seated in his hotel or flat, discussing with his cronies the Upper World's helplessness to protect itself against him. He stops at nothing in his criticism. The " boss," as well as the humblest " flatty," * re-

* Patrolman.

Introductory

ceives freely both his commendation and condemnation. At the bottom of his heart he admires an honest man; deal with him " on the level," and in nine cases out of ten, even though you are not of his world, he will return the courtesy. What makes him angry is that the Upper World builds immense cities, teaches him to be happy only in cities, permits him to grow up as best he can, organizes corrupt police forces to watch him, and then, when he is temporarily down on his luck and cannot pay for favors, sends him to prison, and says: " You be good." Municipal government, as thus administered, he revels in criticising.

The cities about which it has particularly interested me to talk with him are Chicago, New York, and Boston. Last year (1900) I spent three consecutive months in taking his testimony in regard to the management of these different cities. Sometimes he was an old thief who knew all three cities well, and had picked out one of them to end his days in as a tramp; sometimes he was a youngster just starting out on a criminal career; and then again he was an active " professional " whose photograph in the rogues' gallery is still prized. Not all of my informants talked as freely as I should like to have had them; sometimes I was not properly introduced, and they were suspicious of me; but the majority of them

The World of Graft

spoke their minds without reserve. When possible, I asked friends in the police business and employees of the different city governments involved to substantiate or repudiate the alleged facts given me, and in some instances they were inclined to take exception to certain statements, but they generally had to admit that I had got " straight goods."

In regard to the word " graft," which is used freely in the text, I desire to state that it is a generic slang term for all kinds of theft and illegal practices generally. In some cases it also covers transactions which are within the letter of the written law, but wholly outside the law covering equitable treatment of one's neighbor. It is used mainly by tramps, thieves, and thief-catchers, but it is not wholly tabooed in Upper World circles. A " grafter " is one who makes his living, and sometimes his fortune, by " grafting." He may be a political " boss," a mayor, a chief of police, a warden of a penitentiary, a municipal contractor, a member of the town council, a representative in the legislature, a judge in the courts, and the Upper World may know him only in his official capacity; but if the Under World has had occasion to approach him for purposes of graft and found him corrupt, he is immediately classified as an " unmugged " grafter—one whose photograph is not in the rogues'

Introductory

gallery, but ought to be. The professional thief is the "mugged" grafter; his photograph and Bertillon measurements are known and recorded.

The World of Graft is wherever known and unknown thieves, bribe-givers, and bribe-takers congregate. In the United States it is found mainly in the large cities, but its boundaries take in small county seats and even villages. A correct map of it is impossible, because in a great many places it is represented by an unknown rather than by a known inhabitant, by a dishonest official or an unscrupulous and wary politician rather than by a confessed thief, and the geographer is helpless until he can collect the facts, which may never come to light. The most that one man can do is to make voyages of discovery, find out what he can, and report upon his experience to the general public.

PART II

METROPOLITAN GRAFTING

" Chi "—an Honest City

THROUGHOUT the Under World Chicago is known by its nickname, " Chi."*
The word is used more by tramps than by thieves, but it is a familiar term to both. Other cities have similar nicknames. New York is called " York "; Philadelphia, " Phillie "; Cincinnati, " Cincie "; Boston, " Bean-Town "; Detroit, "Slow-Town"; Baltimore, "Balt," and Kansas City, " Kay See." The Under World wants names of its own manufacture for the Upper World cities, and when successful equivalents are found they are incorporated in its language.

The opinions of Chicago as a city of graftdom are many and varied, according to the individual experience of the man who happens to be expressing himself. There are both known and unknown thieves who run down the city and say that they never want to see it again. They have come to grief in some of their undertakings, the " tumble " hurt, and true to their grafter nature they condemn the place for all time. There are also those who claim that it is a profitable field of activity only at certain times; " when a big strike is on," I heard one man say. They have happened to visit the city when there was considerable " doing," and they liked it. At the

* Pronounced " Shy."

[9]

The World of Graft

next visit things were quieter, the " percentage "
detectives were hungry, and the expenses were
greater than the plunder.   Consequently, they
think it is all luck whether a grafter comes out
winner or loser.   To diverse views Chicago is
better in winter than in summer, or the reverse;
more hospitable to old men than to young men,
or the exact opposite; a good lodging-house
town or a poor one, hostile or friendly, " dead "
or " wise."

In April, however, of last year (1900) the consensus of opinion among the grafters with whom
I talked was that Chicago was the best stopping-
place for tramps and thieves in the United States.
To be sure, I interviewed only a small number
of the thousands that are in the city, but they
were so unanimous in expressing the opinion
given that it is fair to assume that they spoke
for the crowd as well as for themselves.   The
best explanation of the city's popularity came
from a tramp called Wyoming Slivers; I mention his name because he does not care.   Some
years ago this man achieved considerable noto-
riety in the tramp world by marrying a well-to-
do widow in Minnesota.   When she died she
left him $10,000 to do as he liked with, and he
elected to invest it in a six months spree in
which all Hoboland was invited to take part.
Slivers came out of the adventure minus three

fingers and an ear, but before it was over ten of his pals lay down and died in different parts of the West.

I found Slivers in the Friendship Lodging-house, off Madison Street. He is a good talker, dresses well—very well for a man who has not done a stroke of work for the last ten years— and is generous with his money, of which he always has a little. In regard to Chicago, he spoke as follows: " I like it 'cause it's honest. The City Hall gang went into office on the promise that the town was to be open, an' they've kept it open. Course they've got to put up a little bluff when the reformers get after 'em, but I know, an' the push knows, that Chi is goin' to be ' right ' for the likes o' you an' me as long as the gang is in power. The reformers can't bluff the gang for a minute. 'T ain't the way 't is in York, where the gang says one thing an' does another. Not on your life. I know exactly how far I can go an' what I can do in Chi, an' that's the reason I feel so at home. It's the same way with the gun* himself. Course he's got to cough up to the coppers ev'ry now an' then, but that's fair enough. You can't get somethin' for nothin' anywhere. If the copper does me a favor, I got to do him one, ain't I? The world's a graft any way you take it. Chi

* Thief.

The World of Graft

ain't no free soup kitchen. The City Hall people want their graft just as much as I do, an' they ain't lyin' about it. To hear the York gang talk you'd think they was all angels. A town ought to be either open or shut, an' the gang ought to say which it's to be. We know what Chi is, an' that's why we hold 'er down."

Although expressed in different words by different men, this is what was said to me about Chicago by the majority of the grafters whose confidence I succeeded in getting. There were some, of course, who thought that the Powers that Rule were not as honest with the Under World on every occasion as they ought to be; I heard a number of harsh criticisms of the police, for instance; but the prevailing opinion was that the municipal government as a whole was about as fair to grafters as civilization at the end of the nineteenth century would allow. No grafter denied that in being fair to his world the authorities were unfair to the honest and hard-working taxpayers. All frankly admitted that the city was "tough" and corrupt, but they declared with equal frankness that they were not in Chicago to reform it. "I take a place as I find it, and not as it ought to be," one man said to me, and he expressed the feeling of his class. In another article will be found the Under World's suggestions in regard to the

things to be done to protect our cities against
" grafters," but they come from men who are
comparatively inactive. Those who are still successfully grafting have but little to say about
reform; actual rather than ideal conditions are
what interests them. How Chicago would seem
with an honest municipal government is, from
their point of view, an academic subject which
it profits very little to discuss. What Chicago
is now and is likely to be for the next six months
or a year, is the vital question to them, and they
discuss it as earnestly as do the politicians.
They are practical, hard-headed men, who want
to know every morning when they get up exactly how far they can go during the day, and
municipal government is narrowed down for
them to the mayor, the police, and the judges
who happen to be in office. These are the Powers that Rule in our cities, with whom they are
most concerned, and they flock to a city or not,
as they are given to understand that their chances
are to be good or bad. At the present moment,
as the Wyoming tramp explained, they consider
their chances in Chicago good, and it is estimat-
ed by conservative observers that they are fully
50,000 strong within the city limits, counting all
the different types.

In talking with them about the city I followed their own method and asked for infor-

mation mainly about the mayor, the police department, and the courts. The City Council was occasionally referred to in conversation, more so, indeed, than in any of the other cities investigated, but almost exclusively in connection with the unknown grafter. It is the opinion of the known grafters that the big " steals " in Chicago are perpetrated by men who are officially recognized as respectable members of the community, and the council was spoken of as an exceptionally well trained " stall " to assist in picking the public's pocket. An old bank burglar with whom I talked, went so far as to say that one of the councilmen used to be a saloon-keeper, in whose care he (the bank burglar) and his pals left their burglar tools between " jobs."

" Of course, I ain't kickin' that ——— ——— has come on so well," the burglar explained; " but it's a little difficult for a fellow like me to think o' squarin' it an' livin' respectable, as the good people say I ought to, when they give me for a city father a man that I know is a grafter. You can't reform nobody by puttin' crooked masters over 'em, an' they'll find that out in this berg some day, too. As things are now, I think I'm more on the level than ——— ——— is. I get out and take my chances like a man, an' 'f I'm caught, I take my trip over the road, an' that's

"Chi"—an Honest City

the end of it. —— —— does all his work under cover. I've been under cover, too, but I
never got myself elected to a town council in
order to hide."

Of the Mayor of Chicago, Carter Harrison by
name, the Under World has but little to say
that is not complimentary. The prevailing opinion is that there is no other chief magistrate of
a town in the United States who has done as
much for "the working classes," and indirectly
for the classes that don't work—tramps, etcetera
—as the present Mayor of Chicago. A pickpocket expressed the sentiment of the grafters
in regard to Mr. Harrison better than anybody
else with whom I talked.

"When Harrison was elected," the pickpocket explained, "he had to choose between
the workin'men an' the millionaires for his push,
and he chose the workin'men. Course he's a
politician an' took up with the workin'men for
reasons that he thought over a long while before he took sides with 'em; but the point is
that he t'rew down the big guys. Ever since
he's been in the City Hall the people 't ain't got
no dough has had a chance. Look at the
tramps that lives here. They come to Chi 'cause
they know that the town's right, that Harrison
ain't goin' to see 'em persecuted. Course the
rich people kick at the way the town's run, but

The World of Graft

that's jus' because they ain't in it. Those street-car gold bugs 'ud 'a' fallen in love with Harrison 'f he'd done what they wanted 'im to do; they got hostile 'cause he passed 'em up. I like him an' the push likes him, 'cause he gives us rope."

To report all that was said to me about the police of Chicago would take a book in itself. In every municipal government it is the police force that 'the grafter knows best and thinks most about, and practically all of his criticisms of the management of a city begin with or drift back to the Front Office. He recognizes that the Front Office is often run by outsiders, such as political bosses, but if you ask him to put his finger on the weak spot in a city's municipal defence, provided there is a weak spot, he invariably directs you to the authorities at police head-quarters. He knows what a police force that is "on the level" can do to keep a city clean, and if it is not clean, it is plain to him that the police department either has orders "from above" not to do its duty, or has refused of its own accord. In the case of Chicago, it is his opinion that the police department consents to the city's being "open," and has an understanding to this effect with the other Powers that Rule. It is part and parcel of an administration that is trying to keep its word with the constituency which put it in power. Naturally, the chief of the force cannot admit this openly; there is another constituency in Chicago which desires that the city be cleaned up, and, minority though it is, the chief cannot afford to insult it. The Under World, however, can read between the lines of the chief's proclamations, and knows that the city is to remain open. As a tramp said to me: " No police force is square with the respectable people of a town that allows as many guns in the city limits as are here in Chi. Wherever you see guns and grafters as strong as they are here you can put it down in your note-book that the police force is grafting." By this it must not be understood, however, that every member of the Chicago police force is " crooked." There are about 2,000 men in the department, and it would be strange indeed if all should be in sympathy with the present régime— there is not enough " graft " to satisfy all, for one thing—but a sufficient number are in sympathy with it to satisfy the Under World critics that the city will never be " shut " while the present city administration is running things.

One of the best illustrations of the indifference of the Chicago police force to the criminal situation in the city, is the freedom with which the " hold-up " and " strong-arm " men conduct their operations. They have " worked " so long

The World of Graft

in Chicago that the city has become notorious as one of their main "hang-outs," and the police apparently make very little effort to apprehend them. Until talking with the grafters who make Chicago their head-quarters, I had been inclined to believe that the "strong-arm" crimes were committed by men who were transients in the city, but I am assured that this is not the case. "They live here, and in the majority of cases are known to the police," one man said to me. "You can give up the other notion, too, that lots of people have, about their being desperate out-of-works. They are professional grafters, every one of them, and I can call the turn on nearly fifty myself." This same informant is authority for the statement that the "hold-ups" in Chicago can be stopped at any time that the police desire to stop them. "The trouble is," he remarked in a conversation about this matter, "that the police don't care whether they're stopped or not. Take a walk some night way out on the south side where a lot of hold-ups have come off, and see how many coppers you'll find. At three o'clock in the morning you'll be lucky if you find one in two miles. They're all in the clear. They don't give a —— about you; they're lookin' for comfort. Even downtown they are likely to be in the clear when you want 'em most. Course I don't care. It suits

[18]

" Chi "—an Honest City

my purposes tip-top; but I'm just tellin' you
why the strong-arm grafters go it so strong."

As contributory evidence of this man's statement about the Chicago police being " in the
clear " when they are most likely to be needed,
I can say that I spent an entire hour in the
neighborhood of Washington Park, on the south
side, one morning about two o'clock, and searched
in vain in street after street for a policeman to
direct me on my way. It is a locality where a
" hold-up " might easily take place, and it was
a matter of wonder to a number of my friends
that I was not relieved of my valuables.

To show how easy it is to find out who the
" strong-arm " men are in Chicago when it is
really desired to discover them, I give here the
names of a few of the West Side grafters of this
character who have " operated " in Chicago off
and on for years.

" Dan " and " Jerry " Kelly	
Daniel Canary	
Michael Casey	
John Ryan	*Pickpockets*
" Paddy " and John Gorman	*and*
William Aherron	*Strong-Arm*
Robert Calendine	*Men.*
" Bill " Braino	
Robert Bruce	
Thomas, *alias* " Bull " Shaughnessy	

The World of Graft

James Barry
"Paddy" Masterson
Patrick Kennedy
Eugene Ryan
William Ryan
John, *alias* "Buck" Troy
John Marshall
"Ed," "Tom," and "Jack" O'Neill
"Bill" Kennedy
George Worington

} *Strong-Arm Men.*

All of these men have had homes within the jurisdiction of the Chicago police, and a trustworthy informant declares that all have received some kind of protection.

George Worington, the last man on the list, and a strong-arm companion, called Kennedy, some time ago held up an elderly gentleman at the corner of Western Avenue and Sixteenth Street, taking away the man's watch and a few dollars. An innocent party was arrested for the crime and bound over to the Grand Jury. In course of time his case came to the notice of an acquaintance of mine, who made an investigation and discovered that the accused party had not been away from his home on the night the robbery took place longer than was necessary to step across the street on which he lived to a saloon, for a can of beer. It so happened that Worington and Kennedy, together with the po-

[20]

" Chi "—an Honest City

liceman who made the arrest, were in the saloon
at the time the innocent man entered it. Worington and Kennedy left almost immediately,
and a half hour after the innocent man had returned to his home the report of the " hold-up "
was announced. The policeman arrested him
as the guilty party, and he would very possibly
have been " railroaded " had not the policeman
foolishly remarked one day, winking significantly
at the same time, that " he knew " who did the
Sixteenth Street hold-up, allowing a certain
party to infer that the man bound over to the
Grand Jury was innocent. The acquaintance of
mine referred to, on getting this information,
notified the policeman, as well as Kennedy and
Worington, that unless the innocent man were
released he would take steps to bring all three
into court. Two days later the accused man was
turned loose, and no more was ever heard of the
matter. I give this case as an example of police
protection, as well as in proof of the league that
so often exists between the police and the grafter.

Another illustration will not be out of place.
In March of last year some copper was taken
from a railroad car standing on a side-track in
one of the Chicago yards. One afternoon the
owner of the copper was notified by the police
that they desired to have an interview with him.
The owner called on the police and learned that

[21]

The World of Graft

they had a "mouthpiece" who thought he could locate the copper if it were made worth his while. The owner refused to enter into any such deal, and the matter was dropped by the police.

A week or so later the "mouthpiece" presented himself at the man's office, and said that he had not only located the copper and the thieves, but had also paid money down to insure the delivery of the copper.

"I can't get you the copper yet, though," he went on to explain, "'cause too many are watchin' the plant, an' the guns don't want to have to divvy with the coppers. When the two fly-cops give up waitin', the guns an' me can come to terms, an' then you can settle with me alone."

At the last account negotiations were still pending between the owner of the copper and the "mouthpiece."

The graft at the police stations is said to run from the lieutenants to the inspectors; but I am assured that a man who has been robbed in a known joint, and goes to the police station to complain, is pretty likely to get his money back when his "pull" is stronger than the joint's. If he is a stranger in the city, and is unable to put up much of a "front," his chances of ever seeing his valuables again are slim. A man, for instance, lost his watch and $90 in cash in

"Chi"—an Honest City

a joint in a certain inspector's district. A friend, with no particular pull beyond a bowing acquaintance with the inspector, called at the latter's office, and tried to interest him in the case.

"Where did you say the man was robbed?" the inspector asked. The place was specified.

"My God! I didn't know there was a joint there." The watch was eventually recovered, but without the help of the police.

In regard to the Front Office men in Chicago, the detectives from "head-quarters," there are nearly as many opinions as there are detectives. Speaking generally, they are not considered particularly "wise." "No up-to-date elbows,* whether they were on the level or not," one man said to me, "would let as many touches come off as these Chicago guys do. Why, you can graft right in front o' some o' them, an' they won't know what you're doin'. I'll bet you ten to one that you an' me could take a walk now through the streets an' see a lot o' graftin', an' yet those Front Office Johnnies 'll make the same trip an' go home empty-handed. There's one fellow up there that ought to be wise, 'cause he rubbered for years when he was on duty in the criminal court; but he's the only one 't I know that's likely to be, an' he may not be up-to-date about the new mugs. To be a wise el-

* Detectives.

[23]

bow you got to keep rubberin' an' rubberin', day an' night, an' you got to know how to rubber. A third-class grafter could give some o' those Front Office people points in the business."

An experience of a friend of mine with an old-time pickpocket will throw light on the policy of the Front Office, as represented by at least three of its operatives. The pickpocket had returned to Chicago from the West, after serving a sentence in prison. He reached the city absolutely penniless. The first persons to recognize him were three detectives from headquarters, and with tears in his eyes he reported to my friend the conversation that took place between them:

" ' How much money you got? ' they asked me. ' Not a red,' I said; ' I just struck town.'

" ' You old liar, you, cough up now, or there'll be a pinch.'

" ' It's God's truth, men, I ain't got the price of a bed in a five-cent lodgin'-house.'

" ' Well, you want to hustle around quick an' get some, an' don't forget that there's three of us.'

" Course I hustled, an' had to pay 'em their percentage; but I told 'em on the level that times was gettin' tough when they wouldn't give an old-timer like me a chance to catch his breath before they braced 'im. If I had all the

money 't I've had to cough up to that kind o'
fellows, I could live in the Auditorium Hotel for
the rest o' my days."

Of the police courts in Chicago there is not
much that I have to report as coming from the
Under World, save the alleged fact that they
are extremely "hungry." One man said to me
that if he were a policeman he would rather
take almost any case to the common police
court than to the Grand Jury, because "the
court has such a big appetite. The judge 'll
fine anything from a nanny-goat to a horse-
block if there's any likelihood o' the fine bein'
paid; an' the Grand Jury may not even indict
in a murder case, on account o' the 'inflooence'
run up against it." An interesting court to ob-
serve is the one at the Harrison Street Police
Station. The professional bail business is carried on here in a way that would prove instruc-
tive even to certain "wise" New Yorkers.

Concerning the different categories of professional thieves to be met in Chicago a great
deal might be written, but the most that I can
attempt here is a very general classification.
The pickpockets—first-class, second-class, and
beginners—constitute probably a third, if not
more, of all the known grafters in the city. It
is reported that there is a syndicate in Chicago
which sends "mobs" of pickpockets all over

the West as occasion demands, but I did not come in contact with any " tool " or " stall " who was willing to admit that he worked under the syndicate's orders. Nevertheless I can understand how a systematized exploitation of the light-fingered gentry in Chicago might be made very profitable, and it is possible that a syndicate has undertaken the task. It is thought by a number of persons that the Chicago pickpocket is the cleverest specialist in playing " the hidden hand " in the United States, but this is one of the conventional Chicago conceits. There are " mobs " of pickpockets working from Chicago that cannot be beaten, but New York produces " talent " equally skilled. A remarkable number of the Chicago pickpockets are youngsters still in their teens.

Another third of the local criminal population is made up of general thieves, boys and men who steal anything that they can conveniently lay their hands on and make away with. A great many of the so-called strong-arm and hold-up offenders are in this category. They are nearly all shabbily dressed and uncouth characters, only a little above the tramp in appearance and manner. Occasionally one of them develops considerable skill in a certain line of outlawry, attracts the notice of some first-class man, and is trained to do high-grade work; but for every one who goes up in the scale, fifty go down. The great majority are what certain detectives call " yegg-men," which is a term, by the way, that the detectives would do well to define. As far as I can discover it means tramp-thieves, but the average tramp seldom uses the word. Hoboes that break safes in country post-offices come under the yegg-men classification.

The remaining third of Chicago's professional thieves are good, bad, and indifferent " sneaks,"* " porch-climbers,"† "slough-workers,"‡ "peter-men," § " prop - getters," ‖ " shovers of the queer,"¶ and representatives of all the other specialties in criminal work. The time has been, and I have no reason to think that it has passed, when a man could go to Chicago and collect as " slick " a " mob " of trained guns as the country contains, and there are organizers of mobs who prefer Chicago talent to any other. As far as I can see, however, it is largely a matter of personal preference and acquaintance, for there are those who have a similar partiality for San Francisco, Boston, Philadelphia, and New York.

The general character of the Chicago gun is more or less similar to that of guns in other

*Sneak thieves.
† Second-story thieves.　　　‡ Country-house burglars.
§ Safe-blowers, bank robbers.　　　‖ Scarf-pin thieves.
¶ Utterers of counterfeit money.

parts of the country; but those who have been
born and brought up in the city—at any rate,
the few with whom I am acquainted—seem to
me to be a little rougher than the Eastern
product.   I think also that they do not set as
much store by fine " togs " as do the New York,
Boston, and Philadelphia guns.   Those who
are in luck dress well, but not so distinctly in
style, it seemed to me, as their Eastern companions.   Socially, they can be as pleasant as
any set of men in the world; indeed, if I were
asked to state the most remarkable quality of
guns of the first class, I think that I should single out their ability to be companionable, when
they want to take the trouble to show their best
side.

I nearly had my " light " put out on one of
my night expeditions in the city, and the man
who, for the moment, would have been glad to
see it go out was a " gun," but it is only fair
to say that on the night in question he was not
in a mood to show his best side.   The trouble
began on account of the word scissors, which I
insisted should be spelled as I have written it;
the gun said that the grammar spelled it " siz-
ors."   An inevitable argument followed, and in
the midst of it the gun levelled his fist at my
face.   I disappeared rather awkwardly, but successfully, and two days afterward the affair was

referred to as " a closed incident " by the gun, and as a close shave by me.

Of the winnings of the thieves in Chicago it is impossible to give any accurate report, but it is a commonly accepted fact, among those who are in a position to know, that the first-class men live luxuriously when they are in funds. By first-class men, I mean thieves who average from $500 to $1,000 a " job." There are first-class pickpockets who are content with $25 a " touch," if the touches come often enough; but the idea is that the skilled men undertake only such work as they are sure will bring good returns. The men with the biggest names and records are not necessarily first-class men. " Blinky " Morgan, for instance, had a reputation in Ohio, some years ago, nearly as great as that of Jesse James, and I had always imagined, until meeting one of his old companions recently in Chicago, that he belonged to the aristocracy of American offenders; but he was considered a second-class man.

" Nervy as they make 'em," his pal said to me, " and a fellow that you could rely on in a scrap; but a bum thief. W'y, I've been up on top o' houses with him at night when I had to lead him ev'ry step he took. He couldn't see. It was his ambition to hold up a train, but he never did it."

The World of Graft

An expert shop-lifter in Chicago can make from $15 to $25 a day; a good porch-climber from $1 to $1,000 a night, just as he happens to strike it; a skilled sneak, anywhere from an overcoat to a thick roll of bank-bills. On the other hand, there come weeks when nothing is realized. The life is extremely precarious, and men who have their pockets overflowing with money one month, are the next month reduced to penury. It is no exaggeration to say, however, that the thieves of Chicago, as a class, have as much to eat as, and probably more spending-money than, the local workingman.

Although the tramp cannot be reckoned in the thief's class, he is such a prominent figure in the life of Chicago that a word in regard to his position in the city will not be inappropriate. In every city he is a good index of the character of the local municipal government. As a general rule, all cities where fakirs show up strong in the streets and tramps have a quarter of their own, are recognized by grafters in general as " open bergs." Chicago is overrun with fakirs, and its Madison Street tramp head-quarters is one of the most notorious hobo nests in the United States. A beggar can " hold down " the city with impunity from one end of the year to the other. I have been in Chicago four times in the last two years, and each time the town was littered up with roadsters from all over the United States. A great many of them barely keep body and soul together, but there are those who take in $5 a day regularly.

I cannot close this chapter without quoting the Under World of Chicago in regard to the local newspapers. I asked one man which paper he thought made the most effort to expose the criminal situation in the city, and his reply gave rise to comments by other informants. It was this man's opinion that no newspaper followed up things after the news editor's sense of a " beat " had been satisfied. " They all just skim over the surface," he declared, " an' they make such a noise about the little that they do publish that the public's got tired. It makes a Chicago business man weary now to chew the rag with him about the ' c'rupshun ' in this city. He's heard and read about it, till he don't want to see the word any more."

Others ventured the statement that no paper in the city would be willing to publish facts about actual deals between the police and the thieves, giving dates and names. " The politicians wouldn't stand for it," they said.

" Any paper," one man declared, " if it wanted to pay the price, which, o' course, would have to be big, could hire some good thief to tell all 't he knows, but it 'ud be afraid to publish his

[31]

story, just because he was a thief. The police an' the politicians have got this town by the neck, an' that's all there is about it. The newspapers can't hurt 'em."

This may be true, but there are certainly "wise" newspaper men in Chicago, and me-thinks that if one of the dailies would give some reporter time enough to follow up an assignment, not merely until the news editor was satisfied, but until a jury would have to convict, an exceptionally interesting "Sunday feature" would be the result.

Summing up the Under World's criticism, as I learned it, of the Upper World's municipal defence against crime in Chicago, the following seem to be the main points: the city is a recognized haunt of tramps and thieves, and where tramps and thieves congregate, by permission, in large numbers, the municipal authorities are not "on the level." It is firmly believed that there exists an understanding between a number of the thieves in the city and some of the detectives, and that it is comparatively easy to make a "spring" out of the clutches of the law when there is sufficient money to hand around to the various persons with "pull." The Pinkerton Detective Agency, it was asserted, could protect Chicago for less than two-thirds of what the municipal police department now costs the taxpayers, and the protection would be real and thorough. When the present administration finishes its operations in the city, it is the opinion of the Under World that a reform administration will be necessary in order to save something for the next City Hall clique to spend.

"York"—a Dishonest City

ONE of the Powers that Rule in New York City, or "York," as the Under World prefers to call it, is a man who used to be one of the Powers that Prey. His photograph as a known thief may still be seen in Chicago, and he is recognized by it, from time to time, when travelling Powers that Rule visit New York. He is generally to be found about eleven o'clock at night in up-town haunts, where he "rubbers" around, makes a "pinch" occasionally, keeps track of new-comers in the haunts, and takes in as much "scale" as his position allows. From the Lombroso point of view, he would hardly be picked out for an "ex-gun." He is intelligent, has good manners, and might pass in the street for an ordinary man of affairs. With those who are able "to call the turn" on him he talks and acts as if his history were known ever since he left the cradle. Until convinced that the "turn" can be called on him, he is likely to be suspicious and uncommunicative.

I met him under circumstances which gave him the right to suppose that his record was known to me, but he was determined to feel me out, if he could, before taking too much for granted. One of the first questions I put to him was: " How are the guns making out here now? "

" We've got the guns pretty well on the run," he replied. I looked at him and smiled. He looked at me in return, and finally also smiled.

" I mean," he said, changing his tone, " that they're leaving town to go to the different resorts. Understand, don't you? "

I nodded my head, and the conversation drifted off into a discussion in regard to the present " system " by which the guns are watched over in the metropolis, and soon after we separated. The man was evidently not comfortable in my company—he knew almost nothing about me—and it did not seem fair to detain him. Furthermore, he said that he had to make a " plant " in a hotel for all night, and he was consequently in a hurry.

I have referred to him, and more particularly to his remark about having the guns on the run, because he is representative of the present police régime in New York City. I do not mean for an instant that the entire police force is composed of ex-guns; the man that I know may be the only one, although the Under World says not; but he is typical in that he wanted to make me believe that the police of New York really have the guns of the city under their control, and are successfully protecting the citizens from them. He knows, his superiors know, and the guns themselves know that New York is, for all practical purposes, as open to grafters as it has been at any time during the last ten years, and it is because the Powers that Rule try to bluff the public into thinking that they are doing their utmost to keep the town shut, when they are not, that the Under World calls New York a dishonest city. It likes New York for some things even more, perhaps, than Chicago, but it is not fooled in the least in regard to the city's official pose as a " closed berg." No one smiles more broadly than the gun when one of the Powers that Rule goes before a Grand Jury or an Assembly Investigating Committee and says that he has no personal knowledge of certain " joints "; and no one is better informed than the gun of how much the Front Office could tell if it wanted to. He does not blame the Powers that Rule for keeping their mouths shut about certain things; if he were chief he would also refuse to enter into details as to why and how certain joints are protected and others are not; but he considers the Powers that Rule silly in making out that they are more righteous than they are. It is his opinion that the public would be much better satisfied if they would come out

" York "—a Dishonest City

boldly and say: " Yes, the town's open, and it's going to stay open as long as the majority wants it open." He believes, as his profession proves, in putting on a bold front and taking chances; men who are afraid to do this and yet graft, be they policemen or politicians, become for him " unmugged thieves."

The blame for the " open " conditions in New York he places virtually where the reformers do—on Tammany. He does not use the word blame; it is not a question of responsibility with him, one way or another; but when asked who it is that secures licenses for the joints and protection for himself when he is able to pay for it, he takes a stroll with you on Fourteenth Street and points out Tammany Hall. By this, however, it must not be thought that he is necessarily a Democrat. Politically he has no real preferences, and if the Republicans were in power in New York, and understood how to manage men as does Tammany, he would make his deals with them as readily as he now does with the " Dimmies." All that he wants is a final authority to which the police, the district attorney, and the courts bow, and with which he can make contracts; cities where this authority can be found he considers absolutely safe. Compared with Chicago, New York is not as available for his purposes as he would like

[37]

to have it—Tammany gets scared every now and then, he says, and has to " throw a bluff " of virtue; but the will to transact business with him is present if the opportunity to do so is not always improved, and his permitted residence in the city is evidence of the fact.

It has been interesting to talk with him about the so-called crusade against vice which has recently caused so much discussion and comment. He has to keep track of such movements in his own interests, and he appraises their value with the precision of a would-be expert. Speaking generally, he thinks that the present excitement in the city concerning corrupt policemen, gambling dens, and disorderly houses, is simply a passing manifestation of public curiosity; that the citizens will get tired before long of the chatter about vice, and the town will then settle back into its customary indifference to such matters. He thinks, furthermore, that he personally has been pretty safe throughout the commotion.

No one knows absolutely how many guns there are in New York; the Front Office itself could not tell for a certainty the number of first-class thieves on the streets at this moment; but it is a generally accepted fact among the guns themselves that every day in the week there are enough grafters in the city to people a good-sized county seat. Collected and classified, the great majority would be found to be rather small fry, but a sufficiently large number of them would have to be included among the A Number One men. They live in the city mainly during the winter, and in the spring " jump out " in " mobs " to the various resorts. There is no doubt that the privilege of having a home within the jurisdiction of the police costs all the first-class men something, but I am not prepared to give any trustworthy schedule of prices. The Power that Rules referred to in the beginning of this chapter is a man who I know could be bribed to keep quiet about a thief's presence in New York, and if I were a thief myself I should not hesitate to offer him $25 when introduced to him, and a " tenner " from time to time during my stay in town. For this remuneration I should expect that he would refrain from tipping me off to his superiors and shield me from orders to call at the Front Office. If he broke faith with me, and I was brought up on the carpet, I should do what a gun of my acquaintance claims is always his practice under such circumstances—" squeal on the copper."

The " joints " where thieves are generally to be seen are scattered all over the city, from the Battery to 125th Street, and even farther up, but a satisfactory tour of their haunts need not extend farther down-town than Bleecker Street

or up-town than Fortieth Street.   Within this
section of the city may be found guns of all ages
and conditions, and it is only necessary to take
a stroll with a gun who knows their faces and
dives, to see them all.   I made one of my inspec-
tions with a little English " moll-buzzer,"* who
claims that he has lived in New York a year and
has not yet been caught or ordered to report at
the Front Office.   His photograph is to be seen
in one of the Western penitentiaries, but courtesy forbids me to give his name or " alias."   His
main graft is picking the pockets of women at
funerals, and he seems to make a very comfortable living; he insisted on paying all the expenses of the inspection.

The majority of the places visited were saloons located on and to the right and left of
Broadway between Fourteenth and Thirty-sev-
enth Streets, but I saw more grafters in " Bo-
hemia," " Cairo," " The " Allen's gambling
house, " Mollie's," in Forty-second Street, and
" The Black Rabbit," in Bleecker Street, than
in all the other places put together.   Only a few
of the grafters were men with " records," but all
of them steal when they can, and the majority
live on plunder.

The life at " The Black Rabbit "—this place
has since been raided—inspired my companion to
make some remarks.

* A pickpocket who robs women.

" York "—a Dishonest City

" There ain't no use talkin'," he said, after we had been sitting quietly at a table for a few minutes, observing the antics of the habitués of the place, " this is dead tough. I wouldn't allow this, 'f I was the chief, I'll be —— if I would. I like an open town where everything goes, all right enough, but I'd douse the glim here. Chapman's* got more gall than I have."

" Perhaps he can't help himself," I suggested. " There may be somebody over at the Hall that stands for it."

" Well, I wouldn't give a —— whether the whole push at the Hall stood for it. I'd put the lights out here as long as I was captain, an' the commissioners could switch me up-town 'f they liked. I'm a thief, an' a bad one, if you like, but no captain o' police has got any business protectin' this kind o' a joint, an' I know it an' you know it. I'd like to see this town run by thieves once. Course they'd graft—couldn't help it—but not any more 'n the police do. Do you know what the coppers cost this berg? Well, it's ten million plunks easy. An' what do the citizens get for it?—the Broadway squad an' a dead easy town to graft in. I ain't kickin' that the town's easy, mind you—not me—but, say, wouldn't you think that the citizens 'ud set-

* Police Captain Chapman was at this time in command of the Mercer Street Station and of the precinct in which the infamous resort mentioned is situated.

[41]

The World of Graft

tle back in the traces an' kick once in a while?
I like York down to the ground, but the citizens are the jayest push o' yaps in this country.
The Londoners are a thick-headed bunch, an' I
don't like 'em, 'f I am English, but they'd no
more stand for what these Yorkers stand for 'n
they'd trade cities."

The majority of the grafters between Twenty-
third Street and Fortieth—indeed, one need not
hesitate to say in the entire city—are those wanderers of the night whom society classifies as
"fallen women." The league between the Powers that Rule and these female Powers that Prey
is founded on the exploitation of the Tenderloin. This district constitutes the most important graft in the entire community, and a gun
is authority for the statement that supreme
control of it is worth a yearly contribution of
$100,000 to the municipal coffers, and a net gain
to the ruler of three times this amount. It would
take too much space to show how the exploitation is managed in detail, but an illustration will
suffice to prove the existence of the league.

One morning, some time ago, a visitor to the
city appeared at the Front Office and reported
that he had been robbed of $80 in an up-town
Raines Law hotel. The man described at the
beginning of this chapter was put on the case,
and in the course of time the guilty party was
found and identified. The case was taken to

"York"—a Dishonest City

court, and the following dialogue took place between the Magistrate and the man who had been robbed:

"You live in Elmira, you say?" the Magistrate asked. The man said that he did.

"What street?"

The man hesitated in his reply, and finally remarked that he preferred not to give the name of the street.

"Is the name you have given your right name?"

"No, sir."

"You're married, I take it?"

The man refused to answer.

"And are a father of children?"

No answer.

"Are you in the custom of coming to New York and going on these expeditions?"

"Not frequently."

"You're sure that the defendant took your money?"

"I had the money last night, and do not remember spending it."

"You were under the influence of liquor, perhaps, and forget what you did."

"I was not drunk, if that is what you mean."

"Could you swear that the defendant took your money?"

"I could not."

The World of Graft

" And yet you think that the defendant did take it? "

" I do."

" You remember voluntarily giving the defendant a certain sum? "

" Yes, sir."

" Was it as much as $80? "

" Most certainly not."

" Could you swear to that? "

" I could."

" How can you prove it? "

" I don't know that I can."

" Then you would hardly be willing to take an oath, would you? "

" I am morally certain that I did not give away the $80."

The Magistrate pondered for a moment, and finally gave this decision:

" As there seems to be considerable doubt in the complainant's own mind in regard to the guilt of the defendant, and as he is unable to swear or prove that the defendant is the guilty party, I am compelled to order the defendant discharged. Woman, you may go."

The detective, who had worked up the case, and a spectator left the court-room together.

" See where the graft is? " asked the detective.

" I see that the defendant got off all right

enough," replied the spectator; "but who gets the coin?"

"I do," the detective declared, importantly, and drew a roll of bank-bills from one of his pockets. "There's the $80."

The most conclusive proof of the existence of a league between the guns and the authorities in New York is that "mobs" of guns are continually leaving the city to do "work" in the provinces, and that the provinces are very seldom warned of their coming.

A man who has been with all kinds of "mobs" in nearly all of the Eastern States, and has always made New York City his head-quarters, declares that the police are in a position to tip off his itineraries to all the world if they want to take the trouble to do so.

"I am known in York," he said to me, "as well as any of the Vanderbilts are, so far as the coppers are concerned, and they can keep track of me through mouthpieces 'way out to 'Frisco. They don't bother me when I'm out on the road 'cause I don't bother them here in town. I fence a good deal o' the swag here, but they don't know where I do it, an' what they don't know they ain't worryin' about. Course they know more 'n they ever let the public think they know; that's good copper doctrine; but the guns can give 'em cards an' spades an' beat

The World of Graft

'em about knowin' what's goin' on. If I leave town lookin' seedy an' come back swell, they know 't I've made a strike somewhere, but nine times out o' ten they don't know where it came off, an' don't care. If I make a touch here in town an' the holler's big, they'll land me 'f they can; but I never done time yet that money wouldn't 'a' got me out of 'f I'd had enough of it. Why, Walling himself, the old Superintendent, said in his book that there wasn't a crime in the calendar that Jay Gould could be convicted of 'f he wanted to pony up enough plunks. It's more or less the same way with a gun. If he's got enough ' fall money ' he can square the whole bloomin' town."

One of the severest criticisms of the detective department of New York that I heard pertained to what a gun described as its " four-flushin' stunts."

" The poor pub swallows the guff ev'ry time, too," he went on. " They make a pinch o' some second-class old thief like Jim Mason, or some o' the have-beens o' twenty years ago, an' tell the reporters that they've copped out the fly- est man on the turf. The reporters go an' chew the rag over again in the newspapers, and the pub thinks that York's got a —— of a cute lot o' elbows. That's what I call four-flushin'. The pub don't hear of a really good gun bein'

" York "—A Dishonest City

copped out in this berg once in six months. Look at the police columns in the newspapers. Nine out o' ev'ry ten pinches is East Side door-mat thieves."

" The pub doesn't hear of many good touches in New York, either," I could not help saying.

" No, if you mean banks an' joolry places; but the Big Man's* protectin' most o' them; 't ain't the Front Office. The guns leave the Big Man's territory alone, if they can. If there was two banks standin' close together, an' one o' them was a member o' the Bankers' Association an' the other one wasn't, the guns 'ud tackle the other one first. The Big Man protects the Bankers' Association banks."

" There are other things to touch up in New York besides banks," I remarked, " yet you don't hear of many big strikes."

" 'Cause you don't happen to hear of 'em, young fellow, don't prove that they don't come off. See? There's leathers, good fat ones, too, lifted ev'ry day in this berg that the pub never hears nothin' about. The guns 'a' got to live, ain't they? Well, they can't live 'less they graft, can they? "

" They can go out of town and graft, and come back here to live."

" That's copper talk. Course there's mobs

* The Pinkerton Detective Agency.

The World of Graft

that don't graft much here in town, but there's lots as do, and you can take my tip for it. Almost every day the papers have a porch-climbin' story to tell, and there's more shovers of the queer in York than in any other town in the country. You just stay here long enough and keep your glims open, and you'll see that this berg ain't backward with its touches."

With all respect to this man's statement, my own observation is that more big " touches " take place in Chicago than in New York. As he well remarks, however, there is no doubt that " fat leathers " are " lifted " and " weeded " in the metropolis practically every day, and the probability is that the majority of them are never recovered.

Of the " boss " of New York I heard more from the Under World than of the boss of any other city visited. Mr. Croker is a subject of never-failing interest to the guns as well as to the politicians and newspaper men, and they discuss his performances and commands quite as intelligently as do Upper World critics. He is by no means so near to them, as a personality, as some of his lieutenants, and I met no gun who claimed that he knew him, but they all understand his power in the city and consider him the chief mogul in the municipal government. The only criticism I heard of him came from a little Irishman, who deplored Mr. Croker's protracted residence abroad.

"The old man ought to stick by the boys better," said the Irishman. "They ain't got the headpiece 't he has, and they're bound to queer things. You don't see Platt runnin' away from his push; he sticks by 'em, whether it rains or shines. That's what Croker ought to do. When a man's boss he ought to stay in his district. Some day the boys 'll make a big mistake 'cause Croker ain't here to tell 'em what to do, an' Tammany 'll get it in the neck. You wait an' see 'f that don't happen."

My other informants spoke of Mr. Croker with considerable reverence, as if he were so high above them that he was beyond criticism. Of his lieutenants, whose names it is not necessary to mention here, I heard things both good and bad, but in the main they were judged friendly to the Under World's enterprises. No one, not even Mr. Croker himself, was considered powerful enough to order the town shut and enforce the order. One man with whom I talked about this matter, said with regard to Mr. Croker: "He might order the town shut, and it might stay shut for a night; but if the boys thought that his Nibs was in earnest they'd turn him down. Croker is boss on the strength of the understandin' that York is to be open and that

The World of Graft

Tammany is to get the benefit of the political graft. If he should go back on his promises to the boys he couldn't remain boss a week."

If Mr. Croker's power is limited, as indicated by this man, his position strikes me as being very similar to that of the Czar of Russia. Theoretically, both men seem to be supreme rulers in their separate spheres, and yet neither one can introduce sweeping changes without the consent of the governed. The Czar of Russia is helpless unless his ministers, officials, and nobles assist him; Mr. Croker, unless " the boys " stand by him. The Under World stands by Mr. Croker because his government of New York City makes grafting easy.

Apropos of the revelations in regard to the Ice Trust in New York, I must quote some remarks of an Under World representative, who made the Trust a text for a long sermon on what he called " Tammany's system of grafting." This man used to enjoy Upper World citizenship; he is to-day one of the best educated gamblers in New York City. I cannot attempt to tell all that he said, but a few of his statements will suffice to bring out his idea.

" The ' boys ' can no more help grafting than they can get out of the Hall. They are all politicians, and they've all seen Richard Croker get **rich**. Some of them knew him when he was

just a beginner. They've watched him get wise
and seen how politics brings money into his
pocket. The majority of them are a lazy, ignorant lot, and when they get into politics it
comes perfectly natural to them to graft. Take
Van Wyck. He's another who's seen how
Croker got rich. That Ice Trust business gives
away the whole story about Tammany and its rich
men. I like to have Tammany run the town, because it helps my trade; but when you ask me
where the big graft in this town is, I've got to
tell you the truth.

"Another fool thing that Van Wyck did
was talking about Parkhurst in that interview.
You remember that he said that Parkhurst went
up to the Tenderloin and paid to see all kinds
of deviltries. What in the world are the deviltries up there for? That's what the citizens ask,
and that's what I ask when a man talks the way
Van Wyck did. Croker ought to teach him
how to talk."

In regard to the gambling places and dis-
reputable "joints" generally in New York, the
Under World declares that the police captains of
the precincts can be held accountable for them.
It is admitted that behind the captains there are
often influential politicians who are the real protectors of the "cribs," but I am assured that
the captains are the men to punish, because the

The World of Graft

" cribs " could not exist without their permission and because they graft off the proprietors. A thief who knows the Tenderloin district well, asserts that a conscientious captain could clean up this district in a week, and the fact that it is not cleaned up is sufficient evidence for him that the local captain is unwilling to undertake the task.

Concerning the courts in New York I heard very little adverse criticism, beyond the statement that complainants in cases similar to the one used as an illustration in the early part of this chapter are likely to be bullyragged and browbeaten. The case referred to certainly proves that one complainant at least was asked some very annoying and very irrelevant questions. The Powers that Prey claim that nine-tenths of the denizens of the Tenderloin are thieves. If this be true, a magistrate is in a pretty poor business when he takes sides in court with a Tenderloin representative charged with theft. The probability is that the accused party is guilty, and the magistrate who favors the defendant in such cases abets both the defendant and the arresting officer in their grafting. Every police-court in New York City where this conniving at crime is permitted is rated by the Under World as " crooked."

The resident thieves in New York represent

the best and the worst of their kind in the
United States. At the present moment there is
perhaps no gang in the city with the reputation
which the old Leslie and Red Leary Gang used
to have; but, as has been stated, a number of
" mobs " work out from New York City, and it
is admitted throughout the gun world that they
are as skilled criminal operatives as can be found
anywhere. In the same streets, however, where
these men may be seen, there are also to be found
bungling " yegg-men " and inexpert beginners.
New York is a Mecca for grafters from all parts
of the country. Young and old, and experienced
and inexperienced roadsters visit it at least once
during their " road " career, and he who has not
yet made the pilgrimage is considered that much
behind his companions in wisdom and general
proficiency. As a lounging place it is not so
popular as Chicago, which, as was stated in the
chapter on that city, is considered the favorite
resort for tramps and thieves; but New York is
certainly next to Chicago in the number of its
local criminals.

At the present moment (February 27, 1901)
as good a graft as any for the pickpockets is the
Brooklyn Bridge. " Mobs " of " dips " can be
found here practically every day, and some of
them are so grasping that they even " switch "
the gold spectacles of old men and women. If

the Front Office would make up its mind to stop
the graft, the Brooklynites could cross the great
bridge with absolute impunity. The local Under World says that the Powers that Rule either
don't want to stop it, or don't know how. The
leader of one of the " mobs " is a notorious thief
who must surely be known to every " wise " operative at police head-quarters, and one of his
" side-partners " is a man who was let loose from
Sing Sing not long ago.

"Cut them out o' the game," is the advice of
certain men who like to talk sometimes about
what New York's police force might do.

The general character of the New York Under World representative is not very different
from that of the Philadelphia and the Boston
criminal, but the New Yorker leads in reputation for skill and " all round " ability. In country towns in the middle West the capture of a
New York thief invariably creates excitement
and arouses curiosity, and the arresting officer
is complimented on his " catch." The man arrested may be known among his colleagues as
a second-rate thief, but the fact that he comes
from New York convinces the local authorities
that they have apprehended a notorious first-
class robber. Not a few guns of the second and
third class have had reputations made for them
in this way. They are always careful, however,

on their return to New York to take their proper place in Under World society; the aristocrats in this society—the first-class men—receive into their ranks no new-comers who cannot prove absolutely their right to be treated as equals.

The profits of a professional criminal's career in New York are as hard to determine as they are in the other cities reported upon. The most that I can say is that the majority of the guns pointed out to me by the little English " mollbuzzer " on the tour of investigation that I made of the guns' joints, were well dressed and seemed to have plenty of spending-money.

As criticised by the professional tramp and thief, New York's municipal defence against crime seems to be faulty in the following particulars: Practically the entire municipal government is at the beck and call of Tammany, and Tammany subordinates the city's interests to its own. New York is " open " because it pleases and pays the Tammany Powers that Rule to have it so. The police department is helpless, because it must obey Tammany's orders and protect Tammany's friends. The guns understand the situation, and feel sure of a domicile in the city so long as they are able to " square " the authorities. If the police authorities were freed from Tammany's rule and were given to under-

The World of Graft

stand that they must clean up the city or give way to men who can, the Under World declares that New York could be " scrubbed out " in two nights. There would still be some guns in the city, but they would have to manage without the aid of the police, and would probably be " railroaded " when caught committing crimes.

The Under World is of the opinion that the citizens of New York do not want the city " scrubbed out," else they would overthrow Tammany. It thinks that much of the talk about the need of reform is pure " guff "—that it does not represent the rank and file of the voters. This is the main point of its criticism of the local defence against crime. The people want an " open " city, and would be the first to complain if it were closed. " There are a few sore-heads," one man remarked to me, " who chew the rag about corruption an' the way the town's run, but they don't represent you an' me an' the citizens. They're sore 'cause they ain't got any offices; that's what's troublin' them. The citizens have got just what they voted for an' wanted, an' they're the only people that can change things. Ain't that right? "

I had to admit that in the final analysis it was the voters who decided whether New York should be " open " or " shut."

Boston—"A Plain-Clothes Man's Town"

ACCORDING to the testimony of living witnesses, some of whom took part in the crusade, Boston became quite concerned about seven years ago in regard to the vice in the city and the men and women who make vice their professional pastime; and a number of raids, arrests, fines, and imprisonments were the result. So far as I know, it is not contended by anyone that all were taken into custody and punished who should have been; nor is it denied that some who were arrested and sentenced are to-day back at their old haunts; but it is pretty generally believed in Boston's Upper World circles—at least I am so informed—that vice received a set-back in the capital of Massachusetts in 1894 from which it has not yet recovered. The first man with whom I talked about my errand in the city said to me: "I have read your paper on Chicago, Flynt, and I want you to understand that you're going to have a regular spiritual bath here compared with your Chicago experience. You'll find Boston a pretty clean city." A spiritual bath differs doubtless in different towns, and is in every town a *Geschmacksache*,* as the Germans say, and

* Matter of taste.

[57]

The World of Graft

the term "a clean city" is obviously purely a relative one; but I gladly state here at the outset that on the surface, at least, Boston looks as if it were trying more strenuously to be good than either New York or Chicago. A tramp in New York, to whom I made practically this statement after my return from Boston, thinks that I confuse the relative value of moral struggles. "P'raps Bean-Town ain't so rotten as Chi," he said, "but that ain't the point. Ye say that Bean-Town is throwin' her feet harder than Chi tryin' to be good.

"Let's call Bean-Town Jim and Chi Jack, and let's say that they both drink. Jack drinks all he can get and whines for more, and Jim, he drinks all he can stand and still put up a front. They both drink too much to be teetotalers, but Jim drinks less than Jack.

"Now, let's suppose that along comes a pretty girl called Cecilia—let's call 'er Cissy for short—and both Jim and Jack lose their heads an' feet to her, an' she says: 'Beloved, I likes ye both, but I'll splice with the one that stops boozin' the first.' Follow me freight-train o' thought? Do, eh? Well, then can't ye see that Jim ain't goin' to have to work so hard to be good as Jack?"

"You mean because he drinks less?"

"Sure, that's exac'ly what I mean. A fella what don't booze as hard as the other fella ain't goin' to have to sweat so much quittin'. That's plain, ain't it?"

"But what does all this have to do with Boston and Chi?"

"I thought ye said ye was followin' me freight-train o' thought? It has everythin' to do with Bean-Town an' Chi. Poor old Chi is like the bloke what I called Jack. It don't drink; it soaks. Bean-Town's like Jim; it don't soak after it thinks it's goin' to lose its front. I mean by soakin' cuttin' up gener'ly, o' course. Now, you say Bean-Town beats Chi tryin' to be good, or that it looks that way when you first get your glims on the two bergs. I think ye're nutty. Chi is Jack, you know, an' jumps from jag to jag like a shammywah (chamois, I suppose), as I heard a fella say once, an' I'll bet ye money it works harder tryin' to be good 'tween jumps than Bean-Town does the year round. 'Tain't what ye ain't, or what ye don't do that cuts ice with me; it's what ye shouldn't be an' is, an' what ye do that ye oughtn't to. The fella that's afflicted with this disease an' struggles to get over it knocks the half-good fella strugglin' into a cocked hat."

In giving me this analysis of the situation in Boston the tramp forgot that I spoke only of the first impression which the city makes on a new-comer. This is not saying that a prolonged resi-dence in the city wholly changes this first im-

[59]

pression, but it is true that after a man has explored for a week or two in the South End and West End, the spiritual bath does not seem so probable as the first walk on the Common had indicated. The revolution of 1894 against vice is still felt all over the city to a certain degree, and I found a very different town on this last visit (March, 1901) from the one I used to know as a tramp twelve years ago, but there are to-day, as then, in abundance, disorderly houses, "speak-easies," saloons or " clubs " where liquor is sold long after the permitted time, and tramps. The thieves do not seem to me to be so numerous as formerly; the women of the street, on the other hand, constitute one of the largest armies of the kind that I can recall having seen in a city of 600,000 inhabitants. There are those in Boston who say that it is hardly fair to class their town as a 600,000 city; that it is really a community of a million people, because the adjoining communities, which are for all practical purposes a part of the city, have a population of four or five hundred thousand. Some of these same persons declare that several of the smaller inland factory towns in New England would show up much worse proportionately than Boston in the particular under consideration. I did not go to these smaller inland towns. Boston was the place that I started out to see, and I stand by my state-

ment. The Under World is so impressed with
Boston as a " hang-out " of the people in question
that it frequently refers to it as " The Town of
Women."   A more popular, concise description
of the city, however, in its present attitude toward
the Under World is that found in the title of this
chapter, " A Plain-Clothes Man's Town."   A
plain-clothes man is a detective, or a patrolman
posing as such.   Boston is not overcrowded
either with " fly-cops " or policemen, but the Under World calls it a plain-clothes man's town, because the grafter has to be careful in exchanging
confidences.   In every city he must exercise
some caution; in Boston he must exercise a good
deal, because he never knows when some ama-
teur detective, representing the reformers, may
be put on his track.   An experience of my own
illustrates his feeling of suspicion.

On a certain evening, in the company of a director of the Watch and Ward Society, a corpo-
ration of anti-vice crusaders, I tried to gain entrance to a disorderly house and a so-called club,
both of which a cabman assured us would furnish
us drinks (intoxicating, mind you) after the
eleven o'clock closing hour.   The " spotters " at
the doors turned us down.

The following evening I went alone to the same
places and got drinks after eleven o'clock.   The
only explanation of why I succeeded alone, that

The World of Graft

I can think of, is that the spotter must have sized
me up to be " one of the boys," and had forgotten
my previous call with the Watch and Ward Society director.   It is my misfortune to be sometimes taken by the Upper World for a detective, but the Under World seldom makes this
mistake.   I should suppose that the Watch
and Ward Society director would never be taken
by anyone for a " sleuth "—he neither looks like
one nor pretends to be one—yet the Under World
was afraid of him, could not make him out.

My reason for including Boston among the
cities about the municipal government of which
I desired to have the Under World's opinions,
was this: I wanted to find out whether the New
Englanders at home manage their most important
city better than New Englanders and others manage some of our other large towns.   It is a popular belief, or at least it used to be, that there is
an uncommon amount of common sense in New
England, and it interested me to learn how much
of this common sense prevails in the management
of the local Under World.

The persons that I talked with most while
trying to gather facts were hackmen, the itinerant
observers of " the crowd that passes," who stroll
up and down such thoroughfares as Washington
and Tremont Streets in squads, keepers and in-
mates of illegal resorts, a few so-called " sports,"

" A Plain-Clothes Man's Town "

a professional and rather successful thief whom
I imported from another State in order to hear
him talk, and four or five tramp friends, who
said that they were glad to see me and immediately " braced " me for a loan. It has
been suggested by certain critics in connection with the paper on Chicago that it was
not fair to go to such worthless members of a
community as thieves and tramps, and give
their criticism of Chicago the prominence that
I did. Gentlemen of the critical pens, who is
likely to know more about the graft in a town
than the people who are grafting? If the re-
spected and " unmugged " grafters of any city
will give me a chance at them, and it would
please the sense of propriety of certain people more to hear what such men have to say
than what " hoboes, thugs, and pickpockets
gabble about," I guarantee that the story when
it is written will read very similar to the Under
World's indictment of the same city. There is
no doubt that the Under World can lie prodigi-
ously when it wants to, and it is a good plan not to
accept all that it advances, even when it is making a definite struggle to tell the truth—after a
man gets into the habit of lying he often falls victim to the habit unconsciously—but I have yet
to find more pronounced falsifiers among tramps,
thieves, and outcast women than among corrupt

The World of Graft

policemen, mayors, public prosecutors, and the like. If it is fair for a corrupt policeman to make a public statement to the world, I fail to see the justice of denying the confessed criminal the same right. I fail to see also why the latter's criticism of men, institutions, and affairs may not easily be as correct as that of the former.

It was a hackman who gave me the first account of Boston's goodness and wickedness as he considered them. I approached him first because he greeted me very cordially on my arrival at the South Terminal station, and seemed inclined to talk indefinitely as long as I would make use of his cab. Also because I have found the "cabby" a mine of information in every city that I have visited. Go to Rome, Samarcand, Tomsk, Berlin, Paris, London, or where you will, and if you can find a wise hackman he can put you " next " to more things on more policemen's beats than can any of the policemen singly. The latter keep track of life merely on their respective beats; cabby keeps in touch with it all over a city.

The name of my cabby was Patsey, and he was a father of children and an Irishman.

" Patsey," I finally said to him, " let's take a long ride, see all that's doing, and let's hear you talk about what we see."

" I'm wid ye."

I jumped up beside him on the box, and while

he drove and talked I listened and asked questions.

" No, they ain't got vice really on the run," Patsey began, in reply to a query of mine as to whether " they " had. " Vice don't run very fast anywhere. It stands still sometimes and waits a little, but I never see it really run. Course my business pluggin' around nights ain't so brisk as it once was, but that ain't the fault o' vice. Those —— yaps from the country are to blame for that. They sit up there in the State House an' legislate for us city people. But we cabbies 'll fool 'em a few, bet your next meal on that. If they ever do get vice dead on the run, an' there ain't no money any more for us cabbies what plugs around nights, do you know what I'll advocate doin' ? "

" Couldn't possibly imagine, unless you mean go out of the business."

" Go out o' the business? Never! Why, boy, that's my horse there in front o' ye, an' this 's my cab. That's what them guys out at Cambridge calls invested capital, ain't it? Well, invested capital has got to protect itself when the law won't do it. Ain't them straight goods? "

" Go ahead."

" Well, sir, if them yaps up in the State House goes it too strong, I'll be for callin' a meetin' o' the cabbies an' financin' places ourselves where we can drive people to—that's on the level, boy. Whoa! Say, boy, this is disorderly house number one."

" Course it'll never come to that," he went on after we had resumed our journey, " but I've got my idea ready in case it should; see? "

" Tell me who protects these places, the police or somebody else? "

" Both. There's Bulfinch Street right there in front o' ye; see it? Well, there's three joints in a row there, an' No. 2 stood it out through the big raid. It's got a pull as big as us Irish."

" The coppers don't dare raid it, you mean? "

" Raid it ? D' ye ever hear o' coppers raidin' anythin' they wasn't told to? "

" But they must know about it? "

" If they don't, they're dead ones."

" Do the other city officials know about the joints? " I asked after we had personally visited ten different " clubs " and resorts.

" Sure. That is, some of 'em must."

" Why? "

" Well, take the Police Commissioners. It's their business to see that the police keep the city clean. If they're any good they prob'ly rubber around on their own hook, an' they must see these joints."

" Perhaps they don't rubber."

" If they don't, they're in a class by their lonelies, 'cause everybody rubbers in this town."

"A Plain-Clothes Man's Town"

One of the "clubs" I visited bears the distinguished name of Cabot; it is situated in a small side street near the Revere House. I refer to it in particular because it is doing all that it can to make the "semicolon" liquor law of Massachusetts ineffective. It seems that the authorities in this State interpret the punctuation of legislative bills to suit themselves, and although the present liquor law was meant to close saloons at twelve or later, the courts decided that the punctuation closed them at eleven—a miserable little semicolon is said to be one of the main causes of the trouble—and at eleven they must close. The Upper as well as the Under World, however, often wants a drink after this hour, and the Under World has arranged clubs and resorts so that neither need go thirsty. The Cabot Club was crowded with parched throats that were gradually becoming moistened the night I was admitted, and a "copper" stood on a corner like a pillar of salt only a block away. He may have been asleep.

Speaking generally, the so-called West End seemed to me to be the most flourishing "joint" district in Boston, and I saw just as tough-looking "mobs" of grafters crowding one another in the streets here as can be found in New York. The South and North Ends, however, and the distinctly business section have their share of tramp

[67]

The World of Graft

as well as aristocratic "hang-outs" of a shady character. In none of the various "Ends," as they are called, did I run across much gambling, and I am assured that organized gambling of the sort that has existed in New York and Chicago has been quite done away with. By this it must not be inferred, however, that a man cannot get into an open poker game if he wants to take the trouble to find one, because a party offered to get me into various kinds of games on any night that suited. At the same time the opportunities for gambling are not publicly advertised, and I believe that in this respect Boston may almost be called a "shut" town. So much for what is recognized as and called vice in Boston. A gentleman who has given considerable attention to this subject in a more or less official capacity, for a number of years, said to me, that if I went to Providence, R. I., I could probably see what Boston got rid of in the revolutionary year of '94.

"Whatever Boston can't stand for in the way of vice," he declared, "has moved on to Providence, and you'll probably find exactly what you're looking for in that town. It's reported to be quite a hummer."

I think I found in Boston all the "humming" that it was necessary to find, and the trip to Providence was consequently not deemed essential to my investigation.

[68]

" A Plain-Clothes Man's Town "

Concerning the vagabondish and criminal proclivities of Boston—the professional or "mugged," and the "unmugged" grafters — it was imperative that I should talk with the hobo and the gun personally, and I succeeded in securing moderately complete statements from both. The hobo is known to-day as "Boston Common Slimy." He used to call himself the "Boston Dude," but that was years ago, when he took great pride in fancy clothes and red neckties. I saw him once in Bughouse Mary's "hang-out," when he would hardly speak to me, he felt so important, but his main notion of style now is sumptuous "set-downs"* and a well-filled pipe of "snipe"† afterward. Even if you should find him dressed in newspapers and a blue necktie he would not mind to-day, provided you caught him tucking away the set-down. He has grown old—he claims that he is only forty-two, but he romances—and life is no longer what other people think it is, but what Slimy thinks it is. He frankly confessed to me that he wasn't living his own real life when he was wearing red neckties; he was trying to "fake the feathers of the main guys" in the Upper World.

I found him in Scollay Square gazing interestedly at a dwarf dressed up as a policeman in the hallway of a variety show. I tapped him on the shoulder and said: "Hello, Slimy." He turned

* Meals.   † Tobacco.

languidly around, gave me a haughty look, and replied in a high falsetto voice, with a feigned English pronunciation: " Sir, do you know whom you're disturbing? This is Boston, sir, and not Madison Street, Chi; see? " and suddenly the high falsetto changed to deep bass, the English pronunciation fled to make way for good old Bowery " twang," and he was the Slimy that I knew.

" You've lost your memory, I suppose," I remarked, drawing away from the crowd, he following, but showing no signs of having recognized me.

" I lost some teeth once, but I guess I ain't lost my memory. Say, kid, who are you? On the level."

I reminded him of our former meetings.

" Why, sure enough, yes—yes—yes. Say, kid, where'd you get the front? I'll bet you a pocketfull o' snipe 't you switched them clothes off a clothes-line over in Cambridge. On the level, now? "

" No, I didn't. I'm workin'."

" Workin' ? Lemme see yer hands. Yes, I recognize them hands. You got 'em white out in the Concord ' Reefer-motory '; what? "

" You're daft."

" Come over an' I'll spend a nickel on you for luck."

"A Plain-Clothes Man's Town"

We were soon seated at a table in a neighboring saloon, and there we stayed for the next two hours. When I finally succeeded in fastening Slimy's talk to Boston, he spoke about as follows:

"Course this berg ain't Chi, an' 't ain't 'Frisco either, but *I* can hold it down all right. That bunch that they call the Back Bay ain't stuck on tramps, but neither 's Michigan Av'noo out in Chi; what?

"Whether the Back Bay has anythin' to do with the front that the town puts up? Well, now, lemme tell you somethin', an' you want to remember it, Cigarette, particularly, if you're workin'. The things that I could tell people what's workin' 'ud make a dictionary.

"There's a Back Bay in ev'ry town, ain't there? Sometimes it's like Fifth Av'noo up-town in York an' keeps its mouth shut, an' sometimes it ain't. This Back Bay here in Boston don't shout such a —— of a lot, but it shouts just enough to keep the mayor, the chief, an' the other guys a-listenin'; see? The town 'll never be absoloot'ly shut— dead shut I mean—even if the Back Bay screamed itself hoarse. You can't tell 600,000 men an' women to be good an' think they're goin' to jus' 'cause you say so. All that the Back Bay's shoutin' really does here is to keep the graft from gettin' too rotten bad.

"The Front Office has to keep up a sort o' per-

petual bluff o' virtue, an' the citizens do, too.
Even your old friend Slimy don't cut up here as
bad as in some other bergs. 'Tain't so much
'cause I'm leary of a pinch as it is 't I jus' natur'ly
feel 't I mus'n't let my angry passions go too far
in Boston."

" Do the other 'boes feel the same way? "

" If they got wise headpieces on 'em, they do.
Proportionately there are just as many bums—
mind you, I don't say 'boes, but bums are worse,
I think—here as there are in any other berg
o' the same size. They're pilin' in an' out ev'ry
day in the year, an' the Back Bay couldn't stop
'em even with dynamite. All 't we try to do is to
keep the Back Bay from gettin' hysterical, see?
I beg here, we all beg, an' we slop up ev'ry now
an' then, too, but we don't go it too strong."

" What do you think about Boston's front?
Would you call it an open or a shut town? "

" I'd call it an open town, but not wide open;
savvy? There's 'boes here, there's thieves here,
there's fallen sisters here, an' there's joints what
ain't on the level, an' that means graft."

" Who is behind the graft? "

" Ev'ry city official what knows about it an'
don't shout. If the Back Bay knows about it, it's
behind it, too."

" You really believe that? "

" On the dead level. I'm Slimy the 'bo all

" A Plain-Clothes Man's Town "

right, but I'm dead next to the duties o' citizenship; see? "

" Did you see what Bishop Potter of New York said about this being the only town that had not asked him to come and say something about the reform of municipal government? "

" No, I never see the religious papers. What did the good bishop say? "

" If I remember correctly he was quoted in the papers as I have stated."

" He was, eh? Well, now lemme tell you somethin' else 'bout this berg. You was askin' 'bout the front that Boston puts up. I suppose you mean its front about bein' good. When I was stuck on red neckties, an' thought I knew all about 'em, I never liked to have anybody tell me that I wasn't next to the latest shades o' red. It use to give me a pain all over. It's the same thing with Boston and her goodness. She don't want Bishop Potter to come up here an' tell her 't she ain't next to the latest curves in goodness. Hully gee, no! That goes against human nature. Besides, Boston ain't so bad as York, an' why should she take a tip from her sister wallowin' in the mud? That goes against all kinds o' nature."

" Then you really think that Boston is moderately good? "

" She's both good and bad, but the badness of her badness ain't so bad as the goodness of her goodness. D' you ever hear that song, Cigarette?"

"Never did."

"Well, I got to be switchin' or I'd sing it to you —but, say, when you quit work, come an' see me again, an' we'll chew the rag some more. Keep happy—so long."

The gun with whom I talked was a man whom I shall have to describe without giving him any other name than John Doe. It would pay the Boston police to put this name in a blank warrant and start out to find him, not, however, because they could do anything with him if they located him, but on account of the information he could give them about people whom it would be of service to them to know. So far as I am aware they have never met him so that they knew who he was, and could not give his real name or any of his aliases, but when a man in the Under World tells you to keep his name quiet, it helps the general status of things to grant the request, and I promised to forget my friend's " monaker "* in public. He is a little man, hardly comes above my shoulders, and I am small, too, and he looks a good deal like a college instructor; but his real business in life is " straightforward swindling," as he calls it. I suppose that he has got money out of people, just by talking to them, in at least ten

* Nickname.

" A Plain-Clothes Man's Town "

different countries, and yet he speaks only the
English language. He came on to Boston to see
me, from a neighboring State which shall be
nameless. I took with me to Boston a card of
introduction, which read thus: "This is my friend
—Billy."* I had hoped to find John Doe putting
up at the resort of the man to whom the card
was addressed, but he was nearly 400 miles dis-
tant, and I had to persuade him to come to me,
or go to him. He finally decided to come nearly
to where I was, but not quite. I found him one
Sunday strolling up and down the road in the
wind which blows between the Massachusetts
Avenue bridge and another bridge on the Cambridge side of the Charles River. Cross the river
he would not, not even to get the important letter I had to deliver to him. " I wouldn't be found
dead in that town," was his reply to my invitation
to take some lunch with me in my room at the
hotel. He was dressed tastefully enough to die
anywhere, and I told him so, but nothing would
do but we must walk up and down in the wind
and talk about the city which he would not
enter. Considering that he dislikes the town,
the reader may think that he is not a fair witness
to put on the stand, that what he has to say will

* I understand that a number of politicians pass their friends
on to other politicians with this same countersign. It can prove
very effective in the gun's world at times.

[75]

The World of Graft

be colored by his general objection to there being such a place as Boston at all. I was inclined to cut out his testimony on this ground also, but on looking over the notes that I jotted down in re-gard to it afterward at my hotel, it impresses me as being far less harsh than what one would naturally expect from such a biased person; and I have decided to incorporate it in this chapter. It reads a good deal like the statement of a cautious witness in the court-room.

Q. " Do you believe that the police force of Boston grafts, or not? "

A. " I think some of them graft."

Q. " Who do you think are on the level? "

A. " From all that I can hear a fair propor-tion of the fly-cops are about as straight as you can get them."

Q. " Do you think they're wise? "

A. " I don't think their brains are crowded with wisdom, if that's what you mean."

Q. " Do you think they could cop you out if you went across the river? "

A. " Not unless they saw me with some gun whom they knew."

Q. " Do you think many new guns could come here if their faces weren't known, and no-body tipped them off? "

A. " Sure."

Q. " Do you think they could graft? "

"A Plain-Clothes Man's Town"

A. " I think there could be a lot more grafting done here, yes."

Q. " Why isn't more done? "

A. " One reason is that the town ain't really right. A man isn't sure of what he is going to run up against in the Front Office."

Q. " Yes, but the new guns' faces wouldn't be known, so what does it matter whether the town's right or not? "

A. " There are bound to be pinches if there are many hollers, and I understand that it's hard to tell how much squaring can be done."

Q. " You're sure that some squaring can be done? "

A. " Absolutely. Every town where the police stand for joints stands for some squaring of hollers."

Q. " Even when the holler relates to a good haul? "

A. " Yes, if the copper that's attending to the matter don't get leary."

Q. " Are there many guns in Boston? "

A. " A fair number. Some of the best guns in the country have come out of Boston."

Q. " Can you give me the names of some guns that make Boston their head-quarters now? "

A. " I can give you the names that I know some of them by; they may not be their right ones, or the names that the police know."

[77]

The World of Graft

Q. "Who are they? Give me the names of some dips."*

A. "'Frisky' Martin, 'Billy' Wilkinson, 'The Boston Switcher,' he is also called 'Sammy the Kid'—his real name is said to be James Brewster; 'Cissy' Williams, she's a shoplifter when she doesn't buzz around women; Marie Rambeau, she's a French Canadian, and is another moll-buzzer; 'Mike' Galway, he comes from Portland, Maine, they say; 'Paddy' Quinn, 'Tim' Ryerson—that enough?"

Q. "Do all of these people live in Boston when they are not off on the graft?"

A. "No, I can't say that. You're liable to see them all over the country, but I understand that they drift back to this town every now and then."

Q. "Do you think the police know them?"

A. "I can't tell you. They ought to."

Q. "Are they good guns?"

A. "Not particularly, but they make their living, such as it is, by grafting."

Q. "Do you think Boston is as much of a bank-man's hang-out as it used to be?"

A. "No. Langdon W. Moore lives here, but he's squared it, so I'm told. There hasn't been a good peter-job in the town for a long while."

* Pickpockets.

[78]

" A Plain-Clothes Man's Town "

Q. " Does the credit belong to the Pinkertons or the local police? "

A. " I don't know. There are men on the force that ought to be able to protect the banks, and possibly they're the ones that are doing it."

Q. What do you think of ex-Inspector Cogan's charges against the police? "

A. " I haven't seen them. What are they? "

I showed him a clipping from the Boston *Transcript* of February 27, 1901, which related to a legislative hearing of the day before in regard to the police of Boston. Former Inspector Cogan of the police force was one of the witnesses called, and the following was the most interesting part of his testimony on the day in question:

Mr. Cogan was asked to make specific charges and then give his reasons for them.

" Then," said Mr. Cogan, " I charge that Mr. Clark is a corrupt man, and that he is unfit to represent the city of Boston as police commissioner. I also make the complaint that William B. Watts is unfit to be a police inspector, and ought to be locked up, and that Charles P. Curtis is a dishonest man, a falsifier, and a liar."

Mr. Cogan was asked if he had brought these matters to the attention of the Commission, and he replied that he had; that in the month of April, 1897, he visited Chairman Clark and told Mr. Clark all about the job that had been put up between Police Inspector Houghton and a man named Hunt to rob the Brighton Bank in 1892. " And I told

[79]

The World of Graft

him that because I intercepted the robbery I was being persecuted," added Mr. Cogan.

In response to a question Mr. Cogan stated that he first complained to Chief Inspector Coulter (now deputy superintendent). He did not tell his story to any commissioner other than Mr. Clark. He explained that when he resigned from the department, July 27, 1899, he tried to tell Mr. Curtis about it, but that Mr. Curtis wouldn't hear his reasons for resigning. This, it appears, was one of the reasons for resigning.

Mr. Cogan said that before calling the matter to the attention of Commissioner Clark he had also confided his information to Chief Coulter, Superintendent Eldridge, and Chief Watts. He told the circumstances of his resignation, a personal matter of discipline with Chief Inspector Watts, which had led to personal feeling. He said that even if matters had been harmonious, he would have been in favor of this bill, as matters have been administered, and indignantly said:

" Why, are you aware that within five years there was a mob of burglars in station 1 ? That the thing was hushed up and the goods were sold at head-quarters? Why, those men have been promoted since then. One committed suicide, and one of them has not only been promoted, but is in line for further promotion."

Continuing, Mr. Cogan said that Officer Walter Murphy, of Brighton, did an exceptionally good piece of detective work in the case of the bank job. There were three professional thieves, but they were followed down to the Revere House, " where three or four inspectors play euchre afternoons."

Mr. McNary—Do you mean to say tnat there

[80]

were burglars in station 1, on the police force; that
the stolen goods were sold at police headquarters;
and that arson was committed by members of the
police force?

" Yes, sir; why, certainly. I can give the names
to the governor and council if they desire them.
The Brighton case was known to Inspector Barrett.
Officer Murphy told of the three men."

" Were those the men who went to the Revere
House to see the inspectors?"

" Most certainly."

Mr. Cogan, in reply to a question, said: " I
think, as a rule, the inspectors of the Boston police
are honest men. I can give names of men, but
I don't want to smirch anybody if this is only to
end in smoke. If the governor or anybody else
agrees to protect these men I will give their names."

Asked if he ever had called the attention of the
Board of Police to this circumstance, Mr. Cogan
said that he had not, because it was no part of his
business as he then considered it.

Mr. Cogan said that he had once enjoyed the experience of taking a professional thief into court,
and of seeing a brother inspector take the stand and
testify that he had known the " crook " for years,
and that he was an honest man.

" Judge Adams," said the witness, sententiously,
" after hearing the testimony, gave the thief six
months." *

* It is particularly agreeable to me to print this clipping, because it shows that the Under World is not the only world that
sees the graft in police life. Critics can, of course, reply that it
is quite as easy for an ex-policeman to throw mud as it is for the
criminal, but I think that this is not a fair answer to the Boston
inspector's charges.

The World of Graft

Q. " What do you think of Cogan's charges? " I repeated after John Doe had read them.

A. " I told you that I believed there was grafting going on in Boston, didn't I? "

Q. " Yes, but do you think Cogan is going it too strong? "

A. " I think he's something of a sorehead, but soreheads can tell the truth sometimes."

Q. " Over in Boston they're inclined not to take him very seriously. Some newspaper men told me this. What do you think in that connection? "

A. " The pub never like to believe anything that they don't think they know a —— of a lot about themselves. If I should go across the river and squeal, we'll say, on certain coppers, the pub would throw me down every time. They'd say, ' He's a thief; what does he know about it? ' Cogan they have to listen to a little because he used to be one of their employees. The pub, my friend, like to fix the wickedness in the world according to their own imagination—if they *think* that a certain man, or collection of men, is honest, God bless me, that's the end of it with them."

Q. " Then you believe that the world in general doesn't want to hear of graft that it hasn't already formed an opinion about? "

A. " More or less, yes. For instance, I was talking about a month ago with a friend of mine who keeps a joint over in P. A.* I told her about a Sunday-school superintendent that I knew was a grafter, because I'd had dealings with him when he was chief of police, and we'd been able to make a dicker. What do you think she said? Give it up, eh? Well, she was a rather good talker, and this is what she said: ' John, for Heaven's sake, leave me some ideals. I know that I'm no lady, but don't tear down every good notion that I may have.' "

Q. " What did you say to her? "

A. " ' Mary,' I said, ' you're in a legitimate business compared with that of some people.' "

Q. " What did she say to that? "

A. " Didn't say anything; she just looked solemn."

As a piece of evidence in rebuttal of John Doe's testimony, I deem it my duty to report a rumor to the effect that one of Boston's police inspectors was offered, on a certain occasion, a $20,000 bribe to assist in a deal of graft, and he refused it. It may be only a rumor—it is very difficult to find out whether it is or not—but I am glad to put it on record nevertheless.

Before leaving Boston I had another talk with the gentleman who promised me a " spiritual bath " during my investigation in the city. I told him a little about my finding, and expressed

* Pennsylvania.

the opinion that Boston was not so lacking in known and unknown criminals as the first impression indicated. I also asked him where he would place the blame for any existing laxity in the municipal government of the city. I think my words were: "Admitting that there are these illegal joints in the city, and that there is probably a fair amount of crookedness in the Police Department, who is to be jumped on before such conditions can be changed?"

"The lazy good people in the Back Bay—in the town generally."

"How do you explain that?"

"If So-and-So, and So-and-So," etc., and he mentioned the names of certain Boston people who are famous all over the world for good works, literary and otherwise, "would band together and say that this town must be clean, the rest of the public would rally around them and make it so. Goodness is lazy in this town, and that's the reason that badness is active." Please note that this is an Upper World statement.

Now, what does the Under World have to say? Practically the same thing. I agree with my friend Slimy that you can't merely tell 600,000 people to be good and expect that they will follow your instructions, but if you should ask Slimy the same question that I put to the gentleman just quoted, he would answer it, in a different idiom, almost

exactly as the Upper World representative did.
The more I learn about the Under World the
more I am convinced that in matters of reform it
has notions and principles very similar to those of
refined people. Slimy doesn't want Boston reformed, and consequently he has nothing to say
about how it could be, but his criticism of the
present more or less " open " city, if put in words,
would state that there is no serious determination
to have it shut—serious determination, I mean,
on the part of those who would be influential in
keeping it shut.

My position is more pessimistic than that of
a number of the Under World critics. I can't
imagine a large city in this country so reformed,
no matter who should bring about its regeneration, that in it I could not gamble, find illegal
resorts and guns, hear of good " touches," and
occasionally run across a crooked official. I have
Under World friends who declare that Boston,
New York, Chicago, and the other large cities can
be absolutely cleaned up if the right people go
about it in the right way. If this be true, then I
ought to be more optimistic—that is all I can say.

PART III

BY WORD OF MOUTH

From One Who Has "Squared It"

WHEN a man who has been a known thief makes up his mind to quit stealing and live "on the level," they say in the Under World that he has "squared it." If he dies in prison before having had a chance to put his new resolution to a test, they say that he has gone "up the escape."

Men change from a criminal life to respectability for various reasons. Some experience a genuine reformation, and prefer to live by honest toil rather than on the proceeds of their criminal practices; others get discouraged and come to the conclusion that the profits in a "gun's" life do not compensate for the losses, and still others find the competition so fierce that they are unable to keep up the pace.

On the outskirts of a city, which shall be nameless, there lives a little man nearing his sixtieth birthday, a member of the class that has found the pace too swift. He has settled down to a quiet existence, contributes $60 worth of service every month to the community in which he lives, and is recognized by his employers as a trustworthy man. Only a few are aware that he has a "record." He has been written about

The World of Graft

in books, and his photograph is scattered far and wide, both in this country and abroad; but his neighbors know him merely as mild-mannered, unobtrusive "Sam." If he should consent to tell them of his wanderings and adventures they would not believe him, he looks so innocent and lives so quietly. Among the majority of the people he meets he is glad not to be recognized as a celebrity. There are those who fail to see in performances such as his genuine enterprise and faithful industry, and it is only human not to want to take people into his confidence about things which he thinks they are unable to understand and appreciate. If properly approached, and sufficient interest is shown, he can be persuaded to talk—indeed, rather likes to—but it must be off in some corner where he can use his own lingo without embarrassment.

Thanks to the kind offices of a common friend, it was possible for me to hear him tell his story, and it let in such a flood of light upon the questions with which my investigation was concerned that I have decided to give it here in full, by way of comment upon what has gone before. As he told it, it seems to me one of the most interesting criticisms of municipal defence against crime as found in the United States that I have been privileged to hear, and my only re-

From One Who Has "Squared It"

gret is that I am forbidden to give the critic's name. His statement, however, is reported exactly as he made it, except in a few instances, when, to shield his identity, it was necessary to change certain names.

"I ain't a reformed man, Flynt, an' can't talk like one, but the Cap says you want me to chew the rag about municipal corruption, as you call it, an' I can give you my side of it, if that 'll do you any good."

"That's exactly the side that I want; go ahead."

"Then I guess I can't do any better than tell you my own story. I'm a Yorker really. 'Course I've knocked about all over, but York has always been my hang-out, an' I go back there ev'ry now an' then an' make a visit. There's a lot o' young ones sprung up since I used to live there, an' I'd have to look over the place again before I could tell you much about them, but I manage to keep track o' most o' the old fellows. I used to belong to Mother Mandelbaum's push.*

"As a kid I was trained to be a machinist, an' it was the learnin' that I got in the machine-shop that helped me to break safes. I wasn't

*Mother Mandelbaum was the most notorious "fencer" New York has ever had. She not only used the police in connection with her business, but was said to run the District Attorney's office as well. She made and lost hundreds of thousands of dollars.

[91]

a peter-man at the start, though; I got to be that after Leslie and Hope took me up.

"I begun as what they call a river thief. A push o' us kids used to own a rowboat on the East River, an' at night, after work was over, we'd prowl around the wharves, hold up somebody, an' then make a get-away in the boat. It was a pretty good graft for young blokes such as we was, an' I made ten times as much dough at night as I did in the daytime in the machine-shop. I was livin' with my old woman at the time, but she never got on to me. She'd 'a' croaked, I guess, if she had. I'm sorry now 't I didn't give 'er more money, but she knew 't I was only earnin' five a week, an' she'd got on to me 'f I'd handed 'er any more. We needed more, God knows, but you see how I was fixed. I used to hide the money 't I made at night in a hole 't I bored in one o' my bed-posts.

"After a while the old woman died, an' I cut loose altogether. If she 'd lived, p'raps she could 'a' kep' me on the level, but I could never 'a' earned more 'n fifteen a week on the level nohow, an' I'd got a taste for luxuries. Understand, don't you? That's what's made me a gun. I wanted a lot o' dough, an' the only way 't I knew how to get it was to steal it. If I'd had an education it might 'a' been different, but I never went to school in my life, an' to-day I

From One Who Has "Squared It"

have to sign my name with an X. That's what keeps me back so now. If I had a trained head-piece on me an' could make good reports, I'd get on; but you can't go to school at fifty-nine an' support a wife, too. I can't anyhow.

"Well, some time after my old woman died, old Hope took notice o' me an' let me into his gang as an outsider. I'd been makin' friends with guns all the while, an' the big guns are always look-in' around for fresh talent. It's just the same as it is in the baseball business. Some manager or captain sees a fellow pitch or catch an' makes up his mind 't he can do somethin' with him. Course Hope didn't set me to crackin' safes right away, but he tried me on the outside part o' jobs. I had to keep watch outdoors while the big fellows was inside gettin' the coin. A fellow that does that an' pipes off places that are to be touched up is called an outsider.

" For the next twenty years after I got to be an outsider I never got arrested, never did a bit o' time an' must 'a' stole well on toward $75,000. An' when they finally did pinch me, it was the Pinkerton people that did it an' not any munici-pal copper. Durin' those twenty years it was the crooked municipal copper that kep' me from gettin' sloughed up, an' I'd be on the turf yet 'f I'd only had him to deal with. As a rule, when the city copper ain't a dead one he's a

The World of Graft

crooked one, an' neither of 'em ever kep' me awake o' nights, 'cause the dead one doesn't know anything, an' the crooked one forgets everything after you've bribed him. See?

"Let me tell you how we used to manage things in New York. If we made a get-away all right an' knew that the police wasn't on to us, course we didn't cough up any coin to 'em; but if there was any trouble about the get-away —if the holler was big—one of us used to go direct to the percentage coppers on the force, tell 'em our tale o' woe, whack up the plunder, an' stop worryin'. That was the system in York twenty-five years ago, an' I know it, 'cause I used to work it myself.

"When Byrnes got to runnin' things, there was a change, but I remember percentage coppers under Byrnes as well as under Walling. Just the same I believe that Byrnes was the wisest, an' takin' him all in all, the best elbow York ever had. I did work in the city after he was inspector, an' he didn't get on to some of it either, but he protected the citizens better than any other man they ever had. While he was at the head the only grafts that ever really flourished, as the papers say, was the Tenderloin, the gamblin' joints, an' the queer,* an' those are all grafts that don't hurt the citizens a bit,

* Green-goods.

[94]

unless they want to get hurt. It's the fellow from the country that they take in, an' Byrnes never put up a bluff about tryin' to protect the countryman. He was in the Front Office to look after the people o' York, an' I'm one o' the old York thieves that thinks he did his job as well as it could be done. I'll never forget how I fooled him once. It was after I'd got pretty well up in the business and was known, an' he use to try to make us known fellows report at his office when we came to town. Generally we reported if there was nothin' pressin' to keep us away, an' I guess the system was a good one, but you got to have dead honest people under you to put it through, an' Byrnes wasn't always lucky in gettin' that kind.

" One day I turned up in the city after doin' a job out in the country, an' one o' the percentage coppers recognized me in Broadway an' tackled me for some dough. I'd never liked the fellow, an' I told him to go to the devil. ' Steal your own money,' I remember I said to him. He thought, you know, 't I'd give him some money to keep quiet about my bein' in town. I ditched him for fair two or three days after, right in the Front Office, too. I'd gone up there to see Byrnes, an' he asked me how long I'd been in town.

" ' About a week,' I said.

The World of Graft

" ' Why didn't you report the day you came in? ' he asked me.

" ' Didn't so-and-so tell you 't I was in town? ' I said. ' I gave him $20 an' asked him to report for me.'

" ' Is that on the level? '

" ' Sure.'

" Course I lied, but Byrnes was better short o' that fellow than with him. I haven't kept track o' things in York since Byrnes was let out, but from all I hear I don't believe things are any better 'n they were in his time. You'll find the percentage coppers there to-day just as I did when he was in the Front Office, and where you find them the public gets it in the neck. Course I know that things ain't the way they were when old Marm Mandelbaum used to live in the city, but I understand that the queer an' the Tenderloin an' the cribs are still the big grafts, an' you can take my tip for it that the police of a town are crooked when such grafts are allowed.

" Do you know who it is in York that I like? Dr. Parkhurst. Tell him that, if you ever see him. Tell him that you know an old York thief, who ain't reformed either as regards havin' a change o' heart, as the church people say, who told you that he considers Dr. Parkhurst the wisest man in the city, barrin' nobody on the police force or off it. He is the one man in the

From One Who Has " Squared It "

berg that you can't fool. I realize better 'n you possibly can what it was that he did when he got Tammany on the run. I've known Tammany ever since I struck the turf; I've been protected by it, an' I've helped protect it; an' I know how strong it was in '94. Now, for one man to overthrow it, as I believe that man Parkhurst did six years ago, is one of the biggest things I know anything about. Mind you, I don't say that 'cause Parkhurst is a preacher, or 'cause I'm stuck on morality. I say it because it was a big stunt, just as holdin' up an express train single-handed is a big stunt. As a gun, I used to like Tammany. Every organization like that makes a town easier for a gun to live in, and if I were on the road to-day an' expected to live in York I'd want Tammany to hold the offices. But, as things are now with me, if the citizens 'ud make Parkhurst chief, an' I could get on the force, I'd work for him on the level— cross my heart, if I wouldn't. He's a whole bunch in himself an' I like him."

He paused for a moment to relight his pipe, and when he spoke again it was in continuation of his own personal story:

" I fell for the first time down South. The tumble hurt pretty bad, 'cause I'd got to think I was never goin' to get caught. Bob Pinkerton copped me out, an' I got a five spot up in

[97]

The World of Graft

Connecticut. I had my choice of a stir* down South or the one in Connecticut, an' I decided to stand trial for the Connecticut job. It was a jool'ry touch, an' the fellow 't I'd done it with turned state's evidence. I ought to 'a' known better than to pal with him, 'cause he was a second-class gun, but I ditched him proper when I got out. He was doin' fence work in York, an' I helped send 'im up the river for eight years. He was the first and last man that wasn't first class that I ever worked with after I got well into the perfesh.

" In '85 I went to England. I made a couple o' pretty good touches, an' then fell hard in Birmingham. It was a jool'ry job again, an' me an' my pal had got into the store all right—it was about seven o'clock in the morning—an' I was standin' near the door peekin' through the letter-box slit an' holdin' the bag for the swag behind me. My pal was fillin' it. Pretty soon a postman came along, an', as luck would have it, he had a letter for the jool'ry store, an' tried to drop it in the slit while my nose was next to it. Course the letter didn't go through, an' the postman kept on pushin' till I got my nose away. We lay low, but the postman had got suspicious, and pretty soon I see two fly-cops go by on the other side o' the street. We tried

* Penitentiary.

[98]

From One Who Has "Squared It"

to make a get-away at the top o' the building, but we found the cops waitin' for us, an' was both caught. We got four years in the same stir that Bidwell was doin' life in for that Bank o' England job. He had it better 'n I did though, 'cause he was in the kitchen where he could get something to eat. I used to be so hungry that I'd pick up the crumbs off the bench after I'd eaten my bread. Those Britishers know how to punish, let me tell you that. If we punished guns in this country the way they do we wouldn't have so many of 'em. I know, 'cause I've done bits in both countries.

"After gettin' out o' the stir I did another job up in Edinburgh, an' came the nearest to gettin' caught without the thing comin' off 't I've ever been in my life. Me an' my pal had shifted to Liverpool after doin' the job, an' as it happened, took a couple o' rooms that two Fenians had just left. We had the swag—mostly diamonds—in our belts, but my pal had left a diamond ring in one of his shoes in the trunk. Two Scotland Yard people knocked at the door one day, an' told us that they wanted to examine our luggage. We didn't know anything about the Fenians havin' been in the rooms, an' was leary as the devil. The coppers found the ring 't my pal had forgotten, an' I thought it was all off.

The World of Graft

"'Where 'd this come from?' they said.

"'It's mine,' I said; 'I carry it there thinkin' it's safer.'

"They took the con, an' not findin' any revolutionary stuff, made up their minds 't we was all right. We fenced the swag over here.

"In '91 I went back to Europe again, but didn't do much except try to pipe off a jool'ry place in Havre. There's a fellow in London that sends out mobs to do work on the Continent, an' he asked me to take a look at the Havre place. Well, sir, I never had a queerer experience in my life than on that trip. You see, I can't speak anything but English, an' when I got to Havre an' begun pipin' off that jool'ry place I got so leary 'cause I couldn't understand what the people about me was sayin' that I thought they was talkin' about me all the while, an' I'd go miles out o' my way, thinkin' they was pipin' me off."

"Did you go up on the hill to the convent where there's a fine view of the harbor?"

"God only knows where I went. All I know is that I took rides on every street-car they got, tryin' to dodge people 't I was crazy enough to think was watchin' me. In London I wouldn't 'a' been a bit leary, but I'd never been in a place before where I couldn't understand the lingo, an' I got so bughouse 't I never finished my job.

From One Who Has "Squared It"

I was to find out how the jool'ry place was protected an' make a report, but all I was able to
tell the boss in London when I got back was
that there was no burglar wires. He never
asked me to go to France again.

"I came back here in '93, an' made up my
mind to try an' square it. I was gettin' old, my
way o' openin' was out o' date for the new safes,
my dough was all gone, an' I thought I'd better
settle down. The only thing 't I could do an'
earn any money was bein' a fly-cop, an' I got a
job. Things went along pretty well for a couple
o' years, an' I was makin' my forty a week,
when an old pal came to me an' asked me 'f I'd
help him open up an old express peter* down
in Louisiana. There was five thousand in it, he
said, an' it was easy to break. Course I was a
fool to listen to him, but, Flynt, an old thief
can no more stand prosperity than he can do
time an' not be glad when he's turned loose.
I'd been livin' good, you know, havin' reg'lar
feed an' the like, an' the old thought about makin' a number one strike an' winnin' out came
back to me. I thought if we could get that five
thousand we could shift to Australia, where my
kind o' business was still rather new then, make
a pile, an' then come back here an' live on the
level. If my pal hadn't had a girl down in New

* Safe.

[101]

The World of Graft

Orleans 't he wanted to see before we left for Australia, p'raps things 'ud 'a' gone the way I hoped, 'cause we got the five thousand all right an' made a clean get-away. I kep' the dough an' my pal went to New Orleans, but he hadn't been there more 'n a day when he was copped out on suspicion. They put him in the sweat-box,* made him cough, an' you know the rest. After I got out o' the stir, all I had to my name was five dollars an' the bummest suit o' clothes 't I've had since I was a kid. I came here, got this job, an' have been here ever since.

"I say 't I ain't reformed, 'cause it's never been a question o' right an' wrong with me. Course I've always known 't ain't on the level to steal, but, as I told you in the beginnin', I wanted a lot o' money, an' I went after it the best way I knew how. I've worked harder for the dough 't I've got at different times than people know anything about. You asked me whether there is any fascination, as you call it, about stealin'. Not a bit. I've never been happy till the job I was doin' was over an' the swag or the dough planted. It's all rot about there bein' any fun in crooked work. Why, I've had to leave men inside a bank for thirty-six hours without anything to eat or drink 'cause

* A prisoner is put in the sweat-box when he is browbeaten by the police in order to make him divulge secrets in his possession.

From One Who Has "Squared It"

people was watchin' me. Do you call that fun, an' how do you think I felt while the men was cursin' me for not passin' 'em in their nourishment? There ain't a harder life goin' than that o' the first-class gun, an' all I've got to show for mine is fifty-nine years an' pretty good health. Course it don't count for much comin' from one who didn't win out, but I'm here to tell you just the same, after a good long experiment with it, that a criminal life ain't worth what you got to pay for it. It's too swift. There's only one of my old gang that's got any money to-day, an' he's the fellow in London. The rest are all dead or on the hog. Look at Jim Dunlap, who was copped out in Illinois the other day for doin' that bum peter job. He use to be in our mob, an' was recognized as a first-class gun. To-day he's knockin' about breakin' into country stores."

"Why is it that the guns don't save money for old age?"

"They can't do it. When they make a strike the first thing they want to do is to blow themselves, an' that costs money. They want to blow themselves 'cause they never know what day's goin' to be their last. When I'd made a get-away after doin' a job, I was never satisfied till I'd blown in ev'ry dollar. First thing I did was to tog up with the best clothes an' jool'ry 't I could buy. Then I'd go to some town where

The World of Graft

I wasn't known an' have a good time. When my dough was all gone, I'd tackle another job. Ev'ry gun is the same way. He hits it up hard until the coin gives out; then he goes to work again. If he's pinched before the next touch comes off, he has the satisfaction o' knowin' that he had a good time out o' the last touch anyhow. He thinks about it all the while he's shut up, an' when he gets out he goes after some more coin to blow himself again.

"There's one thing that lots o' guns do 't I always was shy of, an' I think now that not doin' it helped to keep me from gettin' caught durin' those twenty years. I never let women into my confidence. The average gun goes an' ties up with a woman on the first good touch he makes. The only woman that ever knew much about me while I was graftin' was old Marm Mandelbaum in York, an' she only knew 'cause she was a fence. I like women, mind you, an' am married now, but they tumble more guns 'n all the coppers in existence. The Bidwell boys fell 'cause they told their wives about that Bank o' England touch. They might be alive an' rich to-day if they'd kept their mouths shut. The trouble with guns' wives is that if they get a grouch on or get jealous, the only thing they know to do is to go an' squeal on their husbands. A copper can get a lot out of 'em, too, before they

From One Who Has "Squared It"

know 't he is a copper. They get to chewin'
the rag careless like, an' the first thing they
know they've told the whole story. A man 't 's
on the level don't care, but a gun can't afford
to have a wife that's a mouth-piece. If a young
fellow that was just startin' out in the business
came to me for advice, I'd tell him not to tie up
with any woman till he'd made his pile, and
never to tell her where his pile came from. I'm
sure that that's what helped to keep me under
cover so long. Ev'ry now an' then I get to
goin' over my recollects an' thinkin' out things,
an' that's one of 'em. Course there was a lot
o' just natural dodgin' an' layin' low, but the
two things that helped most was not fallin' in
love an' knowin' how to touch up the coppers.
Since I've squared it I've picked me out a mate,
but I could touch up a copper still."

" Do you think the cities are any less corrupt
than when you were on the road? "

" From all 't I hear about York, I guess 't a
gun can do business there all right yet, but, as
I told you, I ain't been back there very recently.
Chi is as rotten as it ever was. The place is full
o' percentage coppers. I ain't been in Phillie
for years, but if it's the way it used to be, a man
can make a spring there as well as anywhere
else. Bean-Town I never knew much about, but
it turns out a lot o' good guns, an' there's gen-

[105]

erally considerable doin' where they come from.
I don't see much change in any o' the towns.
The pub's just as ignorant as ever 'bout what
goes on, an' the coppers ain't makin' it any wiser.

" I tell you where I have seen changes though
—the guns to-day know more in a minute 'n I
did in a week. That's a fact. I could no more
get out an' compete with the guns on the turf
now 'n I could stand ten years on my head.
You wouldn't think it, but it's the truth. This
generation o' thieves beats the last one hands
down. Course our push there in York had a
big name, an' the newspapers still chew the rag
about it from time to time, but Leslie, Red
Leary, an' all of 'em was greenhorns, let me tell
you, compared with the guns workin' now. The
pickpockets are swifter, the peter-men are better trained, the sneaks are cuter, an' the whole
gang is better educated. I know it 'cause I have
to keep track of 'em."

" How do you account for it? "

" It's easy enough. The guns come from the
people, don't they? Well, the whole country is
wiser to-day than it was twenty-five years ago,
ain't it? Well, the guns have simply kept pace
with the country. That's the whole story. If
I'd start out now I'd have to begin at the beginnin' an' learn the whole business over again."

He paused again, and seemed to lose himself

in his reminiscences. In a moment he looked up and smiled.

" They say 't a man can't begin anything fresh an' make a success of it after he's reached sixty," he continued, " an' I guess I won't try. I'm satisfied; I've had my fling, an' it's over. I'd like to be back there with you in York this summer an' show you some o' the old dumps where I use' to hang out, but I guess I can't make it. If you ever see anything that puzzles you, go to —— ——, an' tell 'im you're a friend o' mine, an' he'll explain the thing 'f he can. He knows as much about corruption as I do. Wherever you are, remember that if there's guns, cribs, an' a Tenderloin in a town, there's crooked work goin' on. After you've located the guns an' the cribs, just dig down as deep as you can go, an' you'll get wise. That's an old gun's advice, an' the youngsters to-day can't give you any better."

I left him standing in the darkness on a railroad track. As my train pulled out, he shouted after me: " Don't forget what I said about Dr. Parkhurst," and then the train entered a tunnel, and he was lost to view.

[107]

Down the Line

ONE of the courtesies of municipal government in the United States is to extend to visiting detectives and policemen the " privileges " of our towns. It is not a written law that these gentlemen shall be treated as distinguished guests, nor is it customary for the mayor of a city to bestir himself in their behalf; but among the police officials of a community where there is any wickedness to display, it is deemed correct that " visitin' coppers " shall have the way made easy for them while they go down the " Line."

The Line differs in different cities, but it is found in every locality in the United States containing ten thousand souls, and cases are on record where a collection of a hundred souls have considered a Line indispensable to their corporate existence.

Speaking roughly, the Line is a community's Tenderloin, and what is found in this quarter of a large city may be found on a smaller scale in provincial county seats; but in police parlance a trip down the Line implies a general survey of the local criminal situation. The Front Office and its rogues' gallery are first inspected, and then the guest and one of the denizens of the office stroll out into the streets, visiting police stations and "joints" in general. The next morning the guest frequently has a "head on" —also the host—and wishes that he had remained at his hotel and never called at the Front Office, but on his return to his provincial beat he tells the "boys" how he did the "Metropolis."

A short time ago I was for the nonce a visiting police officer in one of our large cities, and one evening I called at the local Front Office, threw down my card on the desk, and said I would like to see the town.

"Anything special you'd like to see?" the officer in charge asked.

"No; just the town, that's all."

"Here, Jim," and the inspector beckoned to one of his "operatives" in an adjoining room. "This is an officer from the West, and I want you to show him around and explain to him how we manage things here."

"Jim" was a well-built, smooth-faced, flashily dressed man about forty-five years old, whom the "wise" would have immediately picked out as a representative of one of two professions—thieving or thief-catching. In penitentiary garb and with his hair cut short, criminologists would have pronounced him a good specimen of the American offender; as he stood in the Front Office with

The World of Graft

the other " operatives," he was obviously one of
the wisest detectives the inspector had. There
was something familiar in his face which made
me think that I had met him before, but on the
evening in question no attempt was made to
prove the suspicion. A man whose business it
is to study photographs and to try to discover
the originals in public thoroughfares frequently
thinks that he recognizes in a casual acquaintance
a resemblance to some man whose track he is
following, but often enough the resemblance per-
tains merely to a composite picture of offenders
which has formed in the policeman's mind, and
is wholly untrustworthy as a basis for cross-
questioning.

Nevertheless, it was my Front Office host,
rather than the Line which interested me in
spending three days of my short vacation in the
large city referred to. The first night was de-
voted by both to fencing. The detective tried to
" feel out " me, and I tried to entrap the detective. It is a poor game at its best, but custom
has made it popular before two eyes of the law
" open up " wide. Crookedness on the part of
one or the other of the men playing the game is
usually what makes it necessary.

The second evening the detective " opened up"
wide. Something had convinced him that I was
" right," or he had made up his mind to take his

chances. It is possible, too, that he shared my haunting recollection that there had been a previous acquaintance which justified straight-forward dealing.

"Put away that coin, Jack," he said in one of the resorts where I was about to pay for the drinks. "You've spent enough already for a Western copper. You boys out on the Coast ain't got the graft that we have. Let me settle the bills after this."

There was the unconcealed gratification of the "free spender" in making the statement, but there was also a genuine good-fellowship behind it. Henceforth the game of "feel-out" would not be necessary.

"Is the graft as good as it used to be?" I asked, unhesitatingly.

"'Tain't what it was before the reformers got after us, if that's what you mean," was the reply; "but we're all payin' the premiums on our life in-, surance pretty regular." And he smiled.

.   .   .   .

It was the third night of my inspection of the Line; the resorts were in full blast, the "crooks" of the town were making hauls and dividing plunder, the captain of the precinct was dozing in his chair, and the detective and I were watching the procession as it passed in and out of the notorious "Klondike." There had been a pause in our conversation, and I was about to break it, when the detective turned around, smiled, and said: " Will you tell me your dreams if I'll tell you mine? "

" Sure."

" Didn't you used to travel under the monaker Cigarette? "

" And isn't your name Big Leary? "

" Shake."

" Say, how long have you been thinking about it? "

" Ever since I saw you in the Front Office."

" Same here. Say, let's go over to Old Marm's an' have a talk."

Big Leary declares that the story he told at " Old Marm's " is a straightforward statement of how he became a detective and a full confession of his performances after getting on the force. It has seemed best to give the story exactly as I got it, without comment. It ran thus:

" Of course, I could 'a' kept on trampin'," he began, " an' there's reasons that might 'a' made it better for me 'f I had, but I wasn't enough of a ' dead one ' to stick to trampin'. You remember when I came back from England after doin' the ten-spot for that bank job, don't you? Well, there ain't no use lyin', that stretcher in that English prison certainly did make my ears ring. They never gave me enough to eat, an' they killed

Down the Line

my nerve shuttin' me up in that dungeon. I ain't squealin', mind you, about gettin' punished an' that kind o' thing, but I want you to understand how I came to go trampin'. I came back here to America an' I saw as well as you see those girls over there that if I did another bank job I'd go to pieces all over, an' I thought the best thing I could do was to go an' hide among the 'boes for a while. 'Course my pals 'ud 'a' staked me 'f I'd gone to them, but I didn't want a stake till I knew what I could do with it, an' I thought 't I could study myself best floatin' around for a few months with the tramps. They're a dead push right enough, but I was dead too, as far as doin' any more good work was concerned, an' I guess they didn't do me much harm. You saw me in Cheyenne, an' you know how I looked an' acted, don't you?

"Well, I held it out with the 'boes for nearly a year, an', one day, I made up my mind I'd write my sister who was livin' here an' see 'f she could get me a job on the level. Her man is pretty strong here in one o' the wards, an' I thought he might get me into some machine shop, 'cause I'm rather well up in machinery—time locks, and so forth "—he could not repress a smile—" an' I was willin' to square it an' go to work.

"My sister, she sent me some dough, an' told me to come home an' talk the thing over. She never knew 't I'd been a gun or done time; she just thought 't I was out of a job. Well, I togged up an' came back here an' loafed around for over two months. The coppers had forgotten me— there was only two 't ever knew me anyhow—an' the guns 't I used to go with was all settled or dead, so I went an' came as I pleased.

"Well, one evening, my brother-in-law, he says to me, ' Jackson '—that's my right first name—' will you take a place on the detective force 'f I go to the front for you? It may lead to somethin' better, an' you'll get a hunderd a month till the somethin' better turns up.' I'd been livin' off him all the while I'd been in town, an' it was up to me to begin to earn some coin, an' I told him ' Yes,' 't I'd take the job 'f he'd get it for me. There's been times since I took the job when I've wished 't I'd stuck to the tramps, but I had the notion, you know, 't I could be on the level even 'f I was a fly-cop, so my brother-in-law, he got me the job, an' I became a Front Office copper.

"Well, that's eight years ago, an' I'm still runnin' in an' out o' the Front Office. For a year there wasn't a squarer copper in the town than I tried to be, an' I pinched swell guns just as quick as I did drunks. Just to show you how level I was, let me tell you some o' the good people I settled. I put Three-Fingered Jack away for

Down the Line

four years, Molly Ann the Gun for two, old Bill
Dobbs for sixteen, Fatty from 'Frisco for eight,
and a big Western mob o' dips—I've forgotten
what they all called themselves—for from one to
six years. Well, you know as well as I do that
a man like me wasn't goin' to settle people like
that unless he'd squared it. The Chief he saw
't I was wise an' up to the business—he didn't
know nothin' 'bout my record, though—an' he
kept raisin' my salary when he could, an' I got
to livin' a little high. You ain't never been a
gun, an' I know it, so you can't understand how
a fellow who has been a gun feels when he begins
to get his fifty a week. It's just the same as it
is with a dog that's been runnin' loose an' starv-
in', when he gets a home an' reg'lar meals again.
I began to feel my oats, as they say, an' think
o' the times when I used to average from seven
to ten thousand a year. If I'd been in any other
business, an' somebody had 'a' been lookin' out
for me the way respectable people look out for
them that they likes, I guess 't I'd 'a' been on
the level to-day; but a man who has been a gun
an' ain't got no one lookin' out for him can no
more keep straight after he begins to feel his
oats the way I did than he can fly. I was dead,
o' course, so far as doin' any more jobs was concerned. I wouldn't 'a' touched a bank with a
hunderd-foot lightnin' rod, but I begun to branch

The World of Graft

out in the business—understand, don't you?"
And again a smile ran over his hard face.

"Mind you, I ain't done a cussed thing since
I been on the force that they could prove against
me in a court o' law. Even when the reformers
got loose an' tried to investigate the department,
they couldn't pile up anythin' against my record;
but, it's God's truth, when I was a known gun,
robbin' banks an' bein' photographed an' shut up
all over the world, in my own mind I was an angel
in Paradise compared to what I think I am now.
You see, I learned to know the kind o' copper 't
I am when I was a reg'lar gun, an', God, how I'
hated him! We used to call 'em percentage coppers—that means that they got their percentage
out o' our graftin's, an' gave us protection in exchange. Well, I guess you'll understand me
when I tell you that the percentage copper is just
about as strong in this town as he ever was. I
said 't I get fifty a week. That's what the town
pays me. The guns an' the girls hand over another hunderd.

"'Course there's two sides to the graft, an' I've
thought 'em both out. If I wasn't a 'dead one'
for the real gen-u-ine old graft I'd be out o' this
job to-morrow mornin'. I got to stay in it—
there ain't another hanged thing 't I can do now.
Sometimes when I'm feelin' rather good I figure
the thing out an' say to myself: 'Why, Leary,

Down the Line

they're all doin' it in one way or other, big an'
little, so why get a grouch on?' An' I'll be honest with you, an open town, the way this one is,
helps business a lot. Take the Line, for instance.
'Course everythin' could be shut up, an' the push
could be made to jump town, but, hang it! the
people in this country are just foolin' when they
talk that rot. They don't really want that kind
o' town any more'n I do. Even the farmers in
the country, with all their chewin' the rag about
the c'rupshun in the cities, 'ud be sore as the devil
if they didn't have a place where they could go
an' blow 'emselves ev'ry now an' then. An' see
how many people 'ud be driven out o' business
if I went it strong an' made the Line hostile. See
the money that the cab people 'ud lose, the laun-
dry people, the places that sells flowers, the the-
ay-tres—yes, an' the landlords, too. Why, this
Line here does a business o' ten million dollars
easy ev'ry year—easy! an' the town gets the benefit of it. So, as I was sayin', when I'm feelin'
rather good I don't see the things so blue as I
seem to now. I'm what your old inspector out
there on the Coast used to call an unmugged
thief, if you like—say, that old man did have the
mugged an' the unmugged guns sized up proper,
didn't he? But why shouldn't there be little unmugged thieves as well as big ones? Ain't I got
a right to graft on the quiet so long as the law

can't touch me, as well as His Nibs has—ain't that right? Not a bit o' dough comes my way that ain't given to me. Take that Moll that was in the police court the other morning. She handed me those eighty dollars. I didn't ask for 'em, an' I wasn't supposed to know that they wasn't hers. Buffalo Red was in here last week with some green-goods. He gave me two hunderd o' good money, an' asked me to forget him when I remembered him—that's the way he put it. Who could ever prove anything against me about that? Nobody.

"Well, I could give you a big earful o' that kind o' talk, 'cause that's the way they all chew the rag, an' I do a little of it myself. There's another thing that some of 'em forgets to mention, too. An unmugged thief—you know what I mean, the gun that ain't known to be a gun— can save money. Before I lost my grip in the bankin' business I must 'a' copped out over a hunderd thousand dollars, an' when I came back from England I didn't have a copper. Since I have been in this business I've planted a cool ten thousand an' my family lives well.

"Didn't know 't I was married, did you? Got as nice a little woman an' two kids as you ever see. I wish you was goin' to stay over for another day, an' I'd take you out to the house. They think I'm on the level." Once again a

[118]

Down the Line

smile—a sickly smile—crossed his face. " That's the mean part of it. I have to keep two bank accounts, one for the graftin's an' one for the dough that the woman saves out o' my salary. She'd go off her head 'f she knew 't I took money from these Molls on the Line. She was brought up straight; don't know nothin' 'bout graftin'. 'Course I'd like to hand my wife all I get, but she'd drop on to my graft 'f I did. I'd like to know what the devil the big unmugged thieves tell their wives when they take home their graftin's. What does His Nibs say, for instance? He must lie like the devil, eh?

" If I thought I could do it well I'd lie, too; but you hate to lie to a woman that you're stuck on an' believes everythin' you say. She an' the kids 'll get the money 'f I croak; I got that all arranged. I keep both the bank-books in a safety-deposit box, an' she knows where the key is in case I should drop off sudden-like. 'Course she'll wonder where the dough came from, but there ain't nobody that can prove that it didn't come right. When I croak, the coppers 'll all put flowers on my grave, an' the kids 'll never have to be ashamed o' their dad. It was a wise guy that thought out this unmugged thief racket. Nearly every mugged thief 't I use to travel with is a tramp now, an' they'll croak tramps. I suppose they think I'm dead. None of 'em has ever recognized me here. I was talkin' with a gun the other day, an' he asked me 'f I ever saw the gun they used to call Big Leary. Said he was a square bloke, an' he had a job he'd like to double up with him on. He wasn't tryin' to feel me out —he didn't know 't I was Big Leary. Well, you may not believe me, but for five minutes I thought about openin' up to the guy an' takin' his offer. I wasn't cut out to be a happy un-mugged thief. My real graft was takin' chances in an open fight. You'll laugh, but I once called an unmugged thief down, an' he was a district attorney too. He'd promised to make a weak prosecution against me 'f I'd tell him where some o' the securities 't I'd got was planted, an' I told him, an' then the thief railroaded me for two years. But I got my rap in on him before we left the court-room. 'You old coward, you!' I yapped at him right in front o' the judge, 'you ain't got the nerve to steal on the level, an' you know you ain't.' He ran out o' the court-room. I'd like to hear somebody say that to me—I'd put his face in." He paused for a moment, and his eyes were fixed on the table.

"By God, I would!" he said suddenly, strik-ing the table with his clinched fist. "For my-self I don't care so much, but those kids o' mine are goin' to have a decent start, an' I'm un-mugged, an' I'm goin' to stay unmugged. I tell

Down the Line

you, Cigarette, there ain't nobody that can prove anything against me. Do you understand? "

.   .   .   .

A month later there appeared in the police columns of the public prints, with the sensational caption of " An Unmasked Rogue," the following " story " :

" The police department is once again in disgrace. A trusted operative of the detective force of ten years' standing met his death last night in one of the Tenderloin resorts under circumstances which prove him to have been an ex-convict and a most unscrupulous police officer. His right name was Jackson Fendors, and he was known by this name at the Central Office, but he was notorious a decade ago, both in this country and in England, as the bank burglar ' Big Leary.' He met his death at the hands of an old confederate in crime, who is now at police head-quarters. According to the arrested man's statement the detective had tried to ' shake him down,' a term of the thief's jargon to describe a police officer's demand for money. It seems that if the money is not forthcoming the discovered thief must leave town or go to the Central Office with the detective. Both Fendors and his assailant are reported to have been under the influence of liquor at the time of the shooting, and both drew their revolvers, but the detective was too slow.

The World of Graft

His companion shot him once in the head and again in the lungs. Fendors' dying remark will doubtless be made use of by the murderer's counsel. ' I deserved it,' he said, and then breathed his last. He leaves a wife and two little boys."

PART IV

INSIDE WISDOM

The Mouth-Piece System

A MOUTH-PIECE is a thief who tells tales to the police about his pals. In New York City he is also called a stool - pigeon. The " profession " generally speak of him as a squealer. In looks and manner he is not very different from the thief who keeps his mouth shut. There are, of course, all kinds of mouth-pieces, as there are also all kinds of thieves, but the average mouth-piece cannot be distinguished from the average gun. When he is in luck he dresses in fashionable clothes and frequents popular resorts; when he is out of luck he prowls about for an opportunity to make a strike. The main difference between him and the gun who never squeals is that when luck is against him he is likely to try to turn it in his favor again by selling information to the Front Office. Sometimes he squares it (gives up thieving) and turns detective, and it is the custom not to call him a mouth-piece after he has openly joined the force, but for all practical purposes he is still a mere turncoat. He continues to sell his knowledge about his former pals for money, and I accept the thief's notion that the man who does this is

[125]

a squealer. There are some very successful detectives employed by municipalities, who used to
be successful burglars and pickpockets, but the
very fact that our municipal governments have
to call on these men for assistance shows how
helpless our police forces are. It is my belief
that it is possible to protect a large city without
buying any information from mouth-pieces or
employing any ex-thieves in the detective department, and the purpose of this chapter is to
criticise the present method of using thief spies
and to suggest a way by which they may be dispensed with. As the American police are now
managed, I frankly admit, and have frequently
stated, that the squealer is an unavoidable necessity; without him it would be very difficult
indeed to ferret out many of the crimes committed; but if the police were made to take
their profession as seriously as the thieves take
theirs, they would not have to fall back on the
thief for aid when a puzzling crime came to
their notice.

The origin of the mouth-piece in American
cities, not to go any farther back in his history,
seems to me to be easily explained. He is the
result of laziness and ignorance on the part of
the police, of uncommonly low instincts on the
part of himself, and of an inborn native American desire to have things done quickly, with-

The Mouth-Piece System

out much regard to consequences or probable effects. It is much easier to have a mouth-piece tell you who committed a given offence than it is to discover the culprit on your own hook; as chief of the force you can sit back in your office-chair while the mouth-piece talks, and when he has finished all you have to do is to send one of your operatives to bring in the offender. Of course you say nothing to the public about how you made the capture or what it cost, and it thinks that you are a very wonderful policeman. Wonderful policemen, men who seem to do things by magic, are very much admired in the United States. At different times in our history there has been the notion about this and that police officer that he could catch anybody whom he started out to find. At the present moment a great thief-finder in one of our big cities has this reputation. An extremely successful detective he certainly is, but I venture the assertion that the mouth-piece is the explanation of a great deal of his magic. He understands the business of persuading a thief to catch a thief, and this is the whole theory and practice of the mouth-piece system. It has been developed in the United States probably as far as in any other Anglo-Saxon country, and is the present basis on which the great majority of our metropolitan police organizations, or rather de-

The World of Graft

tective departments, are founded. I propose to criticise the system from the point of view of the policeman, the thief, and the public. I am indebted to the men whom I met on my recent travels for most of the facts and illustrations given, but it would not be fair to commit them to all the opinions and comments expressed. In the main, however, I think that the thief sees the same faults in the mouth-piece system that I have tried to point out, and, when possible, I have given his own criticisms.

The most striking defects of the mouth-piece system, in so far as it concerns the policeman, are that it tempts the honest police officer to be lazy, it permits the dishonest police officer to graft, and it involves payment to the mouth-piece in return for services rendered. The would-be honest policeman is tempted to be lazy, in that he learns to rely on the mouth-piece for " tips " which he ought to train himself to find out. There is nothing inherently dishonest in accepting information voluntarily offered by a thief, but the trouble is that when a policeman or a detective begins with a thief on this basis it is hard to give up the relationship; and the average officer learns to look to the thief for " wisdom," in place of exercising his talents and becoming " wise " on his own account. There are scores of detectives in the

The Mouth-Piece System

United States who would be at a loss to know
how to secure the detection of a crime if their
mouth-pieces were to go back on them, and yet
they might have become quite as clever and
knowing as their Under World allies had they
only been more industrious and independent
when they first took up with police work. In
time, unless they are very exceptional men—
which they generally are not—they learn not
only to make the mouth-piece do the work which
they ought to do, but also to graft. It is not
necessary here to enter into any long description of the different ways by which dishonest
detectives make money out of thieves; a number of these ways have been indicated in the
chapters on certain cities, and I refer to the
matter again when treating of the known thief's
expense account; the fact must be emphasized,
however, that it is the mouth-piece system which
teaches the detective how to graft. It is but a
step from relying on a thief for one's bread and
butter—and this the detective does when he
looks to the thief for the necessary information
to catch and convict an offender whom he has
been sent out to apprehend—to taking bribes
and a " percentage " out of a robbery. A man
who consorts with mouth-pieces is sure to be
approached, sooner or later, by thieves with
hush-money, and if he takes it, both mouth-

The World of Graft

piece and thief have a hold on him. Then begins a miserable career of accepting favors and paying them back. Eventually the day arrives when both mouth - piece and detective know so much about each other that each tries to put the other out of the way. An old New York criminal told me in Chicago that the natural outcome of every partnership between a police officer and a stool-pigeon is that one or the other finally goes to prison. "They've both been so crooked," he said, "that they're afraid of each other, and the copper tries to settle the squealer and the squealer tries to railroad the copper. I know a copper that's doin' five years now on account of his mouth-piece. The mouth-piece is free, and grafts in York."

The thief comes under the corrupting influence of the mouth-piece quite as definitely as does the policeman, but in a different way. The policeman betrays society, and the squealer betrays his pals. Society, through its representatives, goes to him and says: "Peach on your companions, be just as mean and traitorous as you know how to be in our interests, and we will give you a certain amount of protection." Squealers are born rather than made; very few thieves with any standing in their class voluntarily go back on their fellows; but society, in upholding the mouth-piece system, admits to

the squealer that it knows that he is the scum
of the earth, and confirms him in the belief that
the more he lowers himself the more likely is he
to escape punishment. There are men in criminal life to-day because the police once exploited
them as mouth-pieces; they no longer have the
courage or ability to begin life afresh. Once a
mouth-piece always a mouth-piece, is the theory
of the Under World. Well-known thieves in
the employ or under the protection of the police
may be seen from time to time in the company
of criminals who hate mouth-pieces and the
system they represent, but woe unto them if
they are ever caught alone on a dark night.
The first-class thief is rated a bad man according to the accepted standard of morals; but,
criminal though he is, he cannot abide a traitor,
and he puts a bullet through a professional
mouth-piece's heart with the same satisfaction
that a policeman feels when he kills a mad dog.
A high sense of honor, such as the world expects a gentleman to have, is not common among
thieves; but among A Number One men, as the
first-class criminals style themselves, professional
loyalty is a *sine qua non*, and the slightest de-
fection from it marks a man for the rest of his
days. One of the most successful bank-men
this country has produced spoiled what the " profession " once considered the biggest reputation

of its kind in the world, by one " squeal," and the wonder is that his light has never been put out.

Sometimes the mouth-piece sees it to his advantage to fake service to the police, and really work in secret with the thieves, and then the police get what is called the " double cross " and the public " gets it in the neck," as the tramp says. This is the worst feature of the mouth-piece system from the public's point of view, and it is well that it should be thoroughly understood. Actual accounts of " double cross " proceedings will bring out the facts better than any explanation that I might give.

The chief of police of one of our large cities had in his employ, or rather under his protection, a number of mouth-pieces. There was a fashionable race-course within the chief's jurisdiction, and it was expected of him that he would furnish the management of the races police protection. The chief was believed to be " on the level," and nothing came out in connection with the scandal about his mouth-pieces to prove the contrary; but if ever a man was led astray by unscrupulous squealers it was this thief. He relied on his mouth-pieces for information in regard to the presence of thieves at the races, and they systematically lied to him. He would send them to the race-track

The Mouth-Piece System

to look over the situation, with orders to tip off to his officers all guns found on the premises, and for nearly a week they swore by all that the Upper World considers sacred that there wasn't a gun within a hundred miles of the place. Meanwhile " touches " were taking place every day, and the poor chief's office was besieged by the victims, who demanded that he stop the thieving. Some gamblers were particularly loud in making their " hollers," and threatened to bring about an investigation if the chief did not take immediate action to discover the pick-pockets and " prop-getters." As a last resort, and on the recommendation of the management of the races, a " wise " man from a private detective agency was employed to find out who was doing the " nicking," and why the local police authorities had been unable to stop it. He spent two days looking over the situation, and came to the conclusion that he could not protect the place alone. " Mobs " of guns were scattered all over the premises, and it was impossible for one man to keep track of them. The preliminary survey, however, convinced him that either the chief had mouth-pieces and they were " double crossing " on him, or that his own detectives were crooked, and the following interview between him and the chief took place:

" Have you any mouth-pieces, chief? "

The World of Graft

"A dozen of 'em, but they say that they can't find anybody."

"Are you sure of your own men?"

"I know that they're honest, but they don't know many guns, and that's the reason that I sent the mouth-pieces out with them."

"Well, if you'll take your mouth-pieces off the course, and give me four of your best officers in citizens' clothes, I'll see what can be done."

"But what do you want to get rid of the mouth-pieces for?"

"I think they're double crossing on you."

"How do you mean?"

"They go out to the races, tip off all your men to the guns, so that the guns will know them, and then come back and tell you that there isn't a gun on the track. That's the double cross, ain't it?"

"Do you believe that that is what those duffers are doing?"

"That's my theory."

"All right. To-morrow I'll keep the mouth-pieces away, and we'll see what happens."

The following day the "wise" man from the detective agency took his stand at the entrance to the race-course, and the first "mob" of guns that came in and that he knew, he drew aside and addressed thus: "Guns, I know every bloomin'

The Mouth-Piece System

one of you. You, Fatty, I settled in Michigan six years ago. Nobbsy I pinched out in Denver only last winter. Curly and I had a shootin' match once up in Minnesota, and the other two I've seen in the stir. Now, I'll give it to you men on the level: I'm protectin' this track, and I want all you fellows to know it, and I want you to tell all your friends and all the mouth-pieces. And I want you to know that the first touch that comes off from now on will land every one of you at the Front Office, whether you made the touch or not; I'm goin' to hold you responsible for what goes on here. I know where to find you when I want you, so you just better go and tell the other mobs how things stand, and what's goin' to happen to your mob if any more work goes on. Now you can go in and see the races." Not another " touch " was reported during that season on that particular race-track.

The story of another chief of police and a notorious pugilist will also illustrate the untrustworthiness of mouth-pieces. The pugilist had been touched to the extent of a very valuable diamond pin, which, like most men of his class, he carried on his expansive shirt-front. All men are alike to the gun when there is anything to be stolen, and he relieves the pugilist of his " prop " as readily as he " reefs " the leather of a president of a railroad. Indeed, he experiences an increase of joy in " nicking " the pugilist, because the latter is usually rated " a wise boy " whom it takes considerable *finesse* to fool. The pugilist in question had no sooner discovered the loss of his pin than he went tearing about town in search of it. He called at the Front Office to see his friend the chief. " Mike," he fairly howled in his rage, " I've been touched for my stone. Can you pinch somebody so 's I can punch him? "

The chief allowed that he could probably " pinch " somebody, but he recommended a postponement of the arrest until he had consulted with his mouth-pieces.

" All right, Mike," said the pugilist; " but if you don't get the stone I'm goin' off on a big spree. I feel bad, I do. Ain't felt so worse since I lost my wif'."

The mouth-pieces were summoned to the Front Office and told to bring in the ring inside of twenty-four hours. They said they would try, and the indolent chief took another cigar from his waistcoat pocket and continued his perusal of the morning paper. All that the chief ever learned from his mouth-pieces during the specified time, and in fact to this day, was that " the stone had gone out of town," and could not be located. What the mouth-pieces really did was this: they located the thief who had stolen the diamond, sold it for him to a local "fence," and went on a jaunt to a sea-side resort on their profits in the transaction. The pugilist, on learning from the chief that the diamond could not be found, kept his word and went on the promised spree. About a year later he was in a town in Texas, attending a quiet little game of poker at a public place of amusement, when a well-known thief, whom I will call 'Frisco Ribson, strolled into the room with the pugilist's "stone" in his shirt. The thief had noticed it in the eastern fence's stock of "bargains," had taken a fancy to it and bought it, prepared to defend his ownership of it should the rightful owner be found. The pugilist had no more than seen his long-lost gem, when he gave one jump, and reached with outstretched arms for the thief's person. He was quick, but not quick enough. The thief had him covered with his "cannon" before he could do any damage, and he was eventually arrested on the charge of drunk and disorderly. His diamond, at the last account, decorated an innocent little woman's hair out in Honolulu.

The mouth-piece system is also largely to blame for the league that often exists between the Powers that Rule and the Powers that Prey. In cities like New York and Chicago, where

The World of Graft

there is no doubt that the league is in force, the beginnings of the partnership may be traced back to the early efforts of detectives and policemen to induce thieves to catch thieves. Some of these detectives and policemen start out honestly enough, and with no other thought than to bring offenders to their just reckoning; but, as I have indicated, the thief, be he mouth-piece or not, demands return payment for favors conferred, and it is in making the payment that "the eye of the law" oversteps the boundaries of his jurisdiction and compromises himself, morally as well as legally.

Take an actual case. Jim Randall—a fictitious name—got an appointment on a large municipal detective force through political pull. He knew no more about the business of apprehending thieves than does the average citizen, and still less about securing their conviction and imprisonment; but he had not been able to get a foothold in any other career, and a political friend advised him to take the position. Once in the life, he naturally wanted to succeed, and he studied the manœuvres of his fellow-detectives. Excepting those who had formerly been thieves and knew from actual experience, his companions were as helpless as he in telling how pickpockets and burglars "work." Nearly all had to go to some thief and ask his assistance in dis-

The Mouth-Piece System

covering who committed the different crimes they were detailed to look into. Randall followed the example set him, and was soon making acquaintances among criminals. Every acquaintance he formed was practically a debt contracted. When Slim, or Curly, or Shorty gave him a "tip" about a theft, he was bound by all the laws of etiquette known to Under World representatives to close his eyes in their favor when the right moment came. In three years he became so blind that they could work right in front of him and he would not see them. He knew that he was not on the level, that he was not protecting the public, and that he had no right to the salary paid him, but the "push" did exactly what he was doing, and he could not hold his position comfortably unless he went with the "push." He gradually accumulated a snug little fortune out of the "percentages" handed to him by guns whom he had protected.

One day the city was given over into the hands of the reformers, and a strict chief was put in power in the police department. He called up the detectives in turn, and talked with them. To Randall he said: "Jim, you seem to have made money out of your position. You have horses, I see."

"Yes, I have horses."

"You also keep up quite an establishment across the river."

"That's true, too."

"You sport quite a museum of jewels besides."

"Correct."

"Did you get all these things out of your hundred and fifty per?"

"No."

"How did you get them?"

"I grafted."

"I suppose you know what it's up to me to do, then?"

"Yes, I know what's up to you to do, chief," replied Randall in slow, measured tones; "but before you do it let me tell you what an old conductor once said to a division superintendent. The conductor had grafted off the company, and had horses and jewels and a big establishment, the way I have. The super wanted to discharge him, and the conductor said: 'Mr. Superintendent, you forget that I already have these houses, horses, and jewels. If you put a new man in my place he'll probably be poor, and the company 'll have to pay out another big sum to provide him with the things that I've got.' Chief, it's the same in my case. I had to get wise, and in getting wise I made my little pile. I can afford to be on the level now. The new

The Mouth-Piece System

man that takes my place, in case you discharge me, 'll probably be a dead one, and to get wise he'll have to go to thieves. They'll make him crooked."

The last his friends knew of Randall he was a dog-catcher in San Francisco.

To sum up my criticism of the mouth-piece system, I would say that it is a confession on the part of society that it cannot protect itself against criminals without calling to its aid the very men it seeks to punish. An old offender in New York, a man who has known the thief's world for a long lifetime and has succeeded in " doing " mouth-pieces and has been " done " by them, says practically the same thing. " The good people in this town," he explained to me one evening in a Bowery resort, " want me to reform and be good. They say it's wicked to be a crook, against the law, and all that kind of thing. I tell 'em that I know it's bad and against the law, but I tell 'em also: ' Neighbors, you'll never reform me tryin' to persuade one o' my pals to split on me, and that's what you're tryin' to do when you send out thieves to catch me. If you want me to respect law and society, as you call them, get after me on the level and show me that you're strong enough to do me by your lonely. I don't give a —— for society that can't protect itself against a handful o' thieves without makin' the thieves themselves its policemen.' And do you know what it is? I never met a bloomin' city missionary yet that didn't say that that was straight talk."

What shall take the place of the mouth-piece system for the detection and conviction of crime is a matter which has caused a great deal of controversy in police circles, as well as among those who take a merely academic interest in the subject. There are both policemen and criminals who believe that the custom is so old that it is useless to think of doing without the mouth-piece, that he is an inevitable factor in municipal police life. In my opinion it depends wholly on whether the public is prepared or not to support heartily a police organization in which the mouth-piece has no recognition. If this assistance on the part of the tax-payer can be secured, I am convinced that better service will be rendered by a police force which makes no deals with stool-pigeons, and I have to offer as a plan by which they may be dispensed with, the suggestions of a Western observer of criminal and police life who has had to do with mouth-pieces, in the capacity of a professional offender, for over ten years. I had a long talk with this man in regard to the matters I have written of in this chapter, and I finally put to him this

The Mouth-Piece System

query: " Suppose, John, that you were made supreme chief of the police force, say, of Boston, to-morrow morning—that you had the right to do as you thought best with every man in the department, and that you were answerable only to the public—how would you go to work to get rid of the mouth-piece? "

He hardly hesitated an instant in making his reply:

" The thing to be done is so simple," he said, " that it wouldn't interest the pub, 'cause we Americans have the notion that when you reform the police you got to do something sleight o' hand, or the thing won't go. There ain't nothing sleight o' hand about this thing o' mine; it's just plain simple business.

" Now, I'm chief to-morrow mornin', ain't I? And I want to get rid of the stool-pigeons, and make my men stand on their own footin'? The first thing I'd do would be to find out who was honest an' who wasn't. I've got to know that before I can do anything at all. I'd prob'ly be a month to six weeks findin' out the truth about the important men on the force. When I'd located the dishonest coppers, I'd have 'em up on the carpet, and I'd say somethin' like this to 'em: ' Men, I'm your new chief. There are reports in this office that don't help out your reputations worth a cent. If I get any more reports

The World of Graft

about any one of you, I'll not only discharge the man that's reported, but I'll try to send him to the penitentiary. I hope I won't have any more reports. Good-mornin'.' The next day I'd have all my inspectors and captains, honest and dishonest, on the carpet, an' I'd say this to 'em: ' Men, I'm the new chief o' this force, and as fast as I can I mean to train men who'll be able to know when guns are workin', without goin' an' askin' someone to show 'em the work. In other words, I propose to have a detective department that's made up o' wise guys who are on the level, and who don't have to rely on a squealer for their wisdom. I want the captains to see to it that every patrolman and roundsman in his charge informs himself absolutely in regard to the kind of people who live on his beat, and to get acquainted with every tough mug, crook, and tramp that he knows has a home in his district. And I want a record kept of all these tough characters, and I want to see that record in the captains' reports every week. The inspectors will see to it that the captains carry out this order.'

" I would then have the chief of detectives on the carpet, and I'd talk to him like this: ' Inspector, I'm the new chief o' this police force. You have a certain number of men that come under my direction. Some of 'em are dead,

The Mouth-Piece System

some of 'em are crooked, an' some of 'em are wise and honest. I want the whole department wise and honest. I want you to train your men to learn how to pick pockets, break open safes, climb porches, shove the queer, and generally be good thieves. Every now and then I want you to send one of the men out with a mob an' let him see how the mob works, and learn all the new mugs he can. I want you to experiment with every man on the force in this way, an' I want 'em to go all over the country. In one year from now I want to hear from you that you've got a wise detective department. Good-mornin'.'

"Durin' the year that the detective department 's gettin' wise I'd keep weedin' out the force wherever I thought it needed it, an' I'd keep studyin' the town an' the guns on my own account. At the end o' the year I'd have up on the carpet twenty-five o' the best guns that my men could pick out in the city, an' I'd say this to 'em: 'Guns, there's goin' to be no more mouth-piece work in this berg, an' no more graftin' by the coppers. The police force is goin' to ask no favors o' you, an' 's goin' to give none. You don't need to come up here an' report at all. You're free to live in this town just as long as you like, an' where you like, as long as you're on the level. When I catch you

[145]

off the level I mean to soak you just as hard as I can, an' if I catch anybody lettin' you buy him off I'll do my best to soak him too. The people want the town run this way, an' I'm put here to do it. Good-mornin'.' I'd then have one more talk with the inspector o' the fly-cops, an' I'd say this: 'Inspector, you want to caution your men to notice every new gun they see with a known gun, an' you want to have men out West keepin' track o' the Western mobs. I've read the riot act to the local fellows, an' they'll prob'ly lie low; but they'll try to import some outside talent that your men don't know. Have two or three o' your men out on the road all the time, an' make 'em get in with mobs. Good-mornin'.'

"After I'd got things started the best I knew how, I'd invite the reporters o' the town that I thought was on the level to my offices, an' I'd say to 'em: 'Men, I ask you as citizens o' this town to take an interest in seein' that this police force does what the pub wants it to do. The pub has given notice that the town's got to be cleaned up, an' I've told my men how I want 'em to go to work. You fellows get about the city a good deal and see things that I can't, because I'm only one man, and I ask you to report to me any member of the police department that you think 's crooked. Roast him an' me in your

The Mouth-Piece System

papers first if you think that's the best way, but I'll be dead obliged to you if you'll give me the evidence against him before you publish it. What I'm particularly anxious to have is that there shall be no deals goin' on between the police an' the thieves, an' I tell you all right here that the department makes no use of stool-pigeons an' will fire an' prosecute the first copper found makin' bargains with 'em. I believe that better work can be done on this basis, an' I hope you will take an interest in the changes that have been made. I'm much obliged to you for your call, an' I'll be glad to serve you in any way 't I can. Good-mornin'.' In a few words, that's what I'd do to try to break up the mouth-piece system, an' if the people really wanted what I'd be tryin' to give 'em, an' 'ud stand by me when it came to kicks an' silly criticisms, I believe it 'ud be knocked into a cocked hat."

I am inclined to believe also that if the foregoing suggestions were conscientiously followed, and a determined man were entrusted with the direction of things, the squealer would lose his present position and significance in police life; and I submit my friend's plan as the best that has been brought to my notice.

The Known Thief's Expense Account —What it Costs to be a Professional Criminal

"WHEN a very young man I learned to gamble, and lost all my savings and earnings before I became aware that it was a vice over which I had no control. As I could not earn money fast enough to gratify the passion, I chose a life of crime. I made money very fast, but I could not steal fast enough to feed a lot of hungry licensed thieves, the gamblers, and my family. . . . . . The person who starts out to find honor among thieves has a long journey before him. I made the trip, and I did find honor in this class; but the treachery of others cost me $250,000, twenty years in prison, and the ruin of my family, which was as near and dear to me as the family of any honest man is to him. . . . . . I made a miserable failure with all my caution and experience, as all must do who lead a criminal life."

The above pathetic paragraph, taken from the preface of Mr. Langdon W. Moore's "Autobi-

The Known Thief's Expense Account

ography," furnishes the theme for this chapter.* There are differences of opinion in regard to Moore's skill as a bank robber, but I think it is admitted by all who came in contact with him and observed his "style" of work that he was decidedly one of the first-class thieves of his time. There are those who say that if he had only managed differently—in other words, if he could always have seen ahead and acted accordingly—he might have saved his stealings and been a rich man to-day; but the thief can no more always know the right thing to do than can any other human being. He is a pitiful child of circumstance, and the wonder to me is that he conquers his environment as well as he does. If there was ever a man of whom the world said, "him we will bleed," it is the habitual criminal. From the moment he joins the professional thief's ranks until he tumbles down, a discouraged man, into the tramp's class, he is levied upon for revenue by all kinds of people, and not once in a thousand times, at the end of a lifetime, has he saved enough to pay for a simple wooden box in which to lie when he is dead. Throughout his career people go to him and say: "I need so much

* This book, published in 1893, is to be recommended to those who desire a more complete statement of the known thief's expense account. It is one of the most interesting "human documents" in criminology.

The World of Graft

for having been in love with you," "You must pay me such and such a sum for having amused you," "I expect so many thousands for not telling what I know about you," and "You must give me half of the plunder or I cannot acquit you." So numerous are the demands upon the thief's purse that it seems sometimes to him as if the world had known beforehand of the crime he has committed, and is waiting in the street to mulct him. The world is credited with wanting to be "on the level," with the belief that society cannot exist unless fair dealing and honest purposes prevail, but you preach to an unappreciative audience when you tell this to the professional and hardened thief. "On the level!" he will scream back at you in scorn. "Why, neighbors, the world is so crooked that a large part of it actually has the nerve to ask me to support it. I give daily bread to more of your so-called on-the-level people than you have any idea of. Talk to me about heaven and hell if you like, but don't try to crack up the world. I know too much about it."

The average winnings, or stealings, of a professional thief for a lifetime are hard to determine, but the probability is that the first-class man, and it is he who is mainly under consideration here, steals, in the course of twenty-five years, anywhere from twenty-five to three hundred

The Known Thief's Expense Account

thousand dollars. Austin Bidwell is credited with having stolen during his short criminal career over a million dollars, but he confessed to me, some years ago, during a conversation in Chicago in regard to this matter, that the million dollar story pertained to the " mob " with which he was connected rather than to him personally. Langdon W. Moore, in the paragraph quoted from his book, speaks of $250,000 as his limit, and there are other records of phenomenally large receipts, but my own opinion is that $40,000 is a very liberal estimate of the so-called successful criminal's winnings. This figure, divided by 25, which we will say is the number of years that the criminal is active as a thief, gives a yearly income of only $1,600, but it must be remembered that easily a third, and in some instances fully a half, of the twenty-five years are spent in prison, so that it is probably not incorrect to say that the average first-class man has an income, when he is in the open, of from $2,000 to $4,000 a year.

The expense account of the first-class man may be divided into what may be called " personal " and " business " items. The personal items consist of voluntary outlays which every criminal is glad to make when in luck. Let us say that a thief is married and has a family in which he takes a great interest. It amuses him

[151]

The World of Graft

to have his wife dress nicely and his children happy and well cared for, as much as it does the respectable and honored man of affairs. He is as human in such matters as is the ordinary citizen, and there are homes of thieves in which every effort is made to keep the family together and to see the children well started in life. All this costs the thief a great deal of money, because he is naturally a spendthrift and takes delight in having his family " put up an aristocratic front." In some cases he has been known to let the wife manage the financial affairs of the household, and to hand over to her regularly— that is, when he was not shut up in prison—a liberal sum for current expenses. It is more usual, however, for him to be his own bill-payer, and he satisfies his wife by presenting her every now and then with costly jewels.

When not married, and by married I mean legally a husband and father, the thief is apt to satisfy himself with rather simple bachelor quarters and to spend most of his time in gambling resorts and other like places. I have listened to interesting discussions as to whether this kind of a life costs more than the theoretically quieter existence of a family man, but they have seldom revealed anything sufficiently satisfactory on which to base a trustworthy calculation. Married or not, the thief is a passionate

The Known Thief's Expense Account

gambler, so that this item has to be reckoned in his expense account in both cases. Speaking generally, it is perhaps fair to say that if he is inclined to save, which is very rare, the opportunities to do so are better when he is married than when single.

As a single man he is recognized by the entire Under World as one of the main supports of two outlawed classes of people—the professional gaming-house keepers and the strolling outcasts of the night, who have often become outcasts on account of some thief and for whose sake many a man has entered the ranks of the professional guns. Without the thief, in many communities, these two contingents would find it extremely difficult to hold their own in the struggle for existence, and both complain and scold when business in the gun's world is slack. Take away the gun entirely, the moneyed man of the Under World, and our poorhouses would be overcrowded with people who have only kept out of them through their ability to graft off the " peter-man," the burglar, and the pickpocket.

A pickpocket whom I learned to know in New York philosophized in regard to this matter thus: " Course the people what makes laws can't see it as I do, but I consider myself as much of a philanthropist, as they call it, as the

fellow what gives money to build a steeple for
a church. There's prob'ly twenty people, at
least, that lives off me when I'm in luck, an'
that the charity swells 'ud have to look out for
if I didn't. Ain't that philanthropy? Ain't that
helpin' keepin' things movin'? Take the Tenderloin, for instance. Course the thieves ain't
the only people what gives the Tenderloin a
livin', but if we'd drop out an' help take care of
some other district the Tenderloin 'ud feel it
—— quick. See how many hands our money
passes through up there—an', mind you, it's
the passin' around o' money that makes things
go. Just let me mention a few of 'em to you.
There's the Raines law hotel people for one, the
saloon-keepers, the pugilists, the girls what sells
flowers, the beggars, the gamblers, the Chin-
Chins when we wants chop suey—an' I want
mine reg'lar at midnight. Then there's the
po-o-lice. W'y, them coppers up there in the
Tenderloin couldn't have any diamond rings if
we didn't help to pay for 'em. No, they couldn't.
They'd sit down in the street an' actually cry—
an' they're big men, some of 'em—if we guns
was run off the earth. They're like me—they
believe in the brotherhood o' man an' the sister-
hood o' women. Ask a copper up there some
night what 'ud become o' all the people in the
Tenderloin if money stopped passin' around.

The Known Thief's Expense Account

He'll tell you the truth: 'We'd all go to the pogey.' That's what he'd say.

"Course the good people want us guns stopped passin' dough around 'cause we steal it, but what the devil o' difference does it make who shoves it along, so long as somebody's got to do it? I suppose that I can tell, as well as the charity organization can, where a dollar 'll do some good, an' why shouldn't I have the priv'lege o' placin' it? If I didn't, you might have to, so there you are.

"There's another thing people forgets when they run down us guns. Take the mechanics what builds safes an' the guys that invents burglar-alarms an' all the things what's used to protect locked-up money and jewels. Where the devil 'ud those people be if we guns hadn't given 'em a job? I tell you there's millions o' people kept busy just on account o' us guns. And yet did you ever hear a preacher, when he was chewin' the rag about the Ten Commandments an' stealin', ever give us guns any credit for the jobs we get for people? Never! He just sends us all to hell. I tell you, there's a number o' ways o' lookin' at guns."

In order that the reader may have a better understanding of the " personal " items in the thief's expense account, I give here the items for a day in the account-book of a New York

[155]

The World of Graft

gun, one of the very few Under World inhabitants of my acquaintance who keeps a written record of his daily expenditures. He was only a moderately successful man from the thief's point of view, but when in luck he lived up to the limit of his income. The day to which the items refer was in March, 1897. They read thus:

" Breakfast at ——— hotel.	$0	60
Ten cigars	2	50
Two neckties	3	00
Paid laundry bill	1	97
Couple of games of billiards.	0	50
A treat to the house at ———	8	25
Lunch	1	50
A ride in the Park with Slim	3	00

(The cabby stuck us, and I felt like smashing him, but didn't do it.)

Dropped at T's playing poker, ten dollar limit..	86	75
Dinner with Jess	13	50
Theatre with Jess	5	00

(I'd have taken better seats, but I felt sore about dropping the 86 plunks at T's.)

Lost at roulette after the theatre	10	00
Cab home	1	50
Total	$138	12

" P. S.—Pretty stiff day this, but I'm going to send Jess to the country and that will make it cheaper."

The Known Thief's Expense Account

The reply of a gun to a query of mine in regard to what he would do with $1,000, if it should be his luck to make a "strike" to that amount on the evening of the day of our interview, will also throw light on the thief's personal expense account.

"I'd tog up first, I guess," he said. "I like to buy a new suit ev'ry month when I can. That 'ud cost me from seventy-five to a hundred. Then I'd prob'ly get me a new stone or pearl. Them things is always capital, you know, anyhow, an' they look nice, besides. I guess I'd drop about three hundred on one of 'em. Then I'd take a trip with my wif' to the seaside. That 'ud use up the rest. Travellin' alone ain't so expensive, but when you take your wif' along your dough runs out o' your pocket like water. A thousand plunks won't keep me an' the wif' goin' more 'n six weeks."

"When the thousand was gone, what would you do?" I could not refrain from asking.

"That all depends on how the wind's blowin'," he replied. "Course I got to get out an' hustle for some more dough, no matter what's doin', but I must keep my weather eye open for troubles. As a rule when I'm busted I settle the wif' in some boardin'-house on tick, an' stay by my lonely till I've located some more oof. When I've got another piece of coin planted, I

connects with the fam'ly again, an' takes another turn 'round the circle."

" Don't you ever get tired of trips and want
to settle down? "

" There ain't no real settlin' down for the gun
unless he means to square it, an' even then he's
got to sail mighty close to the wind to get
along. To get any fun out o' his life the gun's
got to live for all he's worth when he's free, an'
keep his health good when he's shut up. All
I think about when I'm in the stir 's 'bout the
turn 'round the circle I'll take with my wif' the
first strike I make after I'm turned loose. The
blowed-in-the-glass gun can no more help thinkin' o' such things when he's sloughed up, than
good people can help thinkin' o' the vacation
they're goin' to have in the summer after workin' hard all winter. Guns is human if they ain't
nothin' else. They got to have their runnin'
loose time. I wouldn't steal a door-mat if I
couldn't blow myself after I'd made a get-away
with it."

The " business " items in a thief's expense account, the funds handed out for " professional "
purposes, constitute another story. It costs
the Powers that Prey fully a half, and some say
two-thirds, of their plunderings from society to
keep up their end of the costs which the league
with the Powers that Rule involves. A thief in

The Known Thief's Expense Account

New York City is authority for the statement that the money which his class pays over in a year to the various Powers that Rule in this country who take tithes from criminals, would be sufficient to pay for the policing of five of our largest cities. It is impossible to determine whether this is an exaggeration or not; my own opinion is that it may easily be the truth; but there is no doubt that our professional thieves are relieved of millions of dollars every year by public officials who protect them in their business in exchange for the money which the thieves give them.

The Powers that Rule with whom the thief has most to do, and to whom he pays the greater part of his corruption fund, are the policeman, the district attorney, the "court," and the "jury-fixer." The criminal lawyer also has his "whack," and a strenuous one it is, at the thief's pile, but he is only incidentally one of the Powers that Rule. Including him, however, for the sake of completeness, in the category of those who graft off the thief, we find that there are five men with more or less official power in every community whom our thieves look upon as possible protectors and abettors. By this I do not mean that every town has a corrupt sheriff, district attorney, and "court" — far from it!—but I do mean that in every town in the United States in which a "good" thief has a " tumble "—is arrested for theft—his first inquiry is whether there is any official in the town whose interest in his case he can secure with a bribe.

Permit me to illustrate this statement with an example or two.

Some years ago a man, who has since left the profession and whose name I consequently will not give, was wanted in three different States on charges of safe-breaking, a bank robbery, and a " pennyweight job " (robbery of jewels). He had been arrested on the safe-breaking charge, and had in his possession at the time a little over $5,000. The State in which he had done the " pennyweight job " was particularly anxious to get hold of him, but his whereabouts at the time of his arrest were not known to the authorities of the State in question, and the authorities who held him in the other State were not sure who he was. It was the man's wish to stand trial in the State which was so anxious to judge him, because he knew that the punishment meted out to criminals in that State for " pennyweight work " was by no means so severe as the punishment in the other two States for safe-breaking and bank robberies, and he sent for a well-known criminal lawyer. The lawyer came—they had met and transacted business before—and the thief addressed him thus: " Bill,

The Known Thief's Expense Account

I've got five thousand plunks, and I want to
stand trial up in York State for the jewelry
racket. Unless they get somebody to turn
state's evidence they can't convict me, and even
if they do they'll hardly give me over three years.
Now, I want you to get the York people on my
track—they have the first whack at me anyhow
—and then quash the indictments in —— and
——. I'll give the York lawyer a thousand for
taking care of me up above, and you can have
the other four thousand for yourself and the
lawyers in the other States. Although they
don't know it, they've got me pretty dead to
rights here, and if I'm railroaded I'll get ten
years sure; so you see why I want to go back
to York State."

" I'll do what I can," the lawyer promised,
and the thief was eventually taken to New York
with the consent of the authorities who held
him; they declared in the newspapers that they
wanted to work up the evidence against him,
and needed the time that the trial and possible
imprisonment in New York would give them.
His lawyer worked hard for an acquittal on the
" pennyweight " charge, and succeeded in con-
fusing the jury as well as the court in regard to
his client's identity, but they decided to give him
a year anyhow on " general principles "—this was
not their official explanation, but the one they

The World of Graft

gave was no better—and the thief went to the
"stir." His friend "Bill" succeeded meanwhile
in quashing the other indictments, and also secured his client's pardon at the end of seven
months. Had justice been done the man in each
of the three States—he was guilty of all three
charges, and his lawyer knew it—he would easily
have had twenty years to serve behind the bars.
For $5,000 and seven months' loss of liberty he
got out of all three scrapes, and at the end of a
year had another bank account.

It is the custom in certain towns, when a big
gathering of people is expected on account of
some reunion or fête, to invite detectives from
other cities to come and help the local police
force protect the crowd. Guns railroad to these
celebrations from all parts of the country, and
the local police cannot possibly know them
all. The visiting officers are called in to tip off
the guns with whom they are acquainted. If
this were the best possible of worlds, and everybody in it preferred an honestly earned dollar to
one that had been grafted, the plan would be a
good one; but the way the world is now managed, it is very difficult to know whether the invited policemen from abroad are honest or not,
and grafting is consequently easy, as the following story will prove:

Two detectives from the West were once in-

The Known Thief's Expense Account

vited to be present at a big patriotic " function " in one of the large Atlantic seaboard cities. They were to receive $100 a piece and expenses for their services and " wisdom." The chief of the local police organization allotted them particular districts to help take care of, and cautioned them to be on the look-out for Western guns. The function turned out to be a great attraction for thieves of all kinds, and in the course of a few days the two detectives met some of the " talent " from their part of the country. The talent had been in the city nearly a week before the detectives saw them, and had succeeded in making some very profitable " touches "; they were nearly all light-fingered gentry. They knew the detectives and their calibre quite as well as the detectives knew them, and there was no hesitancy on their part in shaking hands with them and talking over the situation.

" What's doin'? " one of the temporary " protectors " of the town asked one of the pickpockets.

" Nothin' in particular," was the reply. " Times is hard, you know," he added, with a tortuous wink of his left eye.

" Many leathers come up? " pursued the detective, regardless of the hard-times whine.

" Only a few—just enough to pay for meal-tickets, that's all."

[163]

The World of Graft

" Got any meal-tickets for us? "

The guns looked at one another, and then at the detectives. They knew that it was another bid for " percentage," but they wondered how big the " percentage " was going to be. The spokesman for the detectives did not keep them long in suspense.

" So much down now," he said, " and so much when the show's over. Otherwise it's a tip-off and pinch."

The guns looked at one another again, asked what " so much " meant, and began to take stock of their " coin."

" Two hunderd apiece now," the detective explained " and another hundred apiece when the show's finished."

The guns asked for more lenient terms, but in vain, and the preliminary payment was made. Only the guns know how many " leathers " were lifted afterward in the district which the Western officers were taking care of, but they were able to make the final payment agreed upon when the function ended, and did not complain of being short of travelling expenses for the homeward journey. The detectives were not overwhelmed with congratulations on the way they had protected the territory assigned to them, but the last heard of them they were still in the employ of their home city and were being

occasionally invited to protect other municipal,
ities.

One more illustration: Jervis Willson—this is
not the man's real name, but his real name would
reveal nothing to the reader—and his " mob "
had a " mark "—in their case, an easy bank to
rob—in one of the Northern States. They had
been watching it diligently for several months,
and had settled on a date for doing the job. The
police and two lawyers of a city not far from the
county-seat where the planned robbery was to
take place got wind of the mob's intentions to
the extent that they knew that Willson had his
eye on a bank somewhere in their part of the
State. Recently discovered facts make it certain that they could not have told at the time
whether the bank was in their own town or a
hundred miles away, but it has been definitely
proved that someone tipped off to them Willson's intentions upon some bank in their neighborhood. They were also convinced that if the
" touch " came off, Willson and his mob were
going to have a very handsome " piece of
money " to divide. They tried their utmost to
find out which bank it was that was to be
robbed, and made frantic efforts to persuade
someone to " squeal," but without success. As
a last resort to get something out of the deal, for
it has since developed that their whole interest

in the matter was one of graft, they concocted the following scheme to fleece Willson:

They accused him publicly of being implicated in a bank robbery that had taken place in their own town about two years previous to the time that they published their suspicions of his guilt. He was a man whom it was easy to accuse, because he was known to be a professional bank-sneak and "peter-man," and it was no secret that he had robbed several banks. The evidence of his participation in the robbery in question was not sufficient to extradite him from the State in which he lived, but it was a part of his plan, in connection with the bank to be robbed, to have some of his men "operate" out of the town where he was wanted, and as he knew that he was innocent of the crime charged against him, he determined to clear up matters by voluntarily surrendering himself to the police. It was a silly proceeding, as later events proved, but the man had no idea of the trap that had been set for him. He had hardly been lodged in jail, however, and secured his lawyer, when the whole trick was revealed. His bail was fixed at $8,000, and he had to furnish it himself in cash; he was a professional criminal, and no citizen was willing to stand sponsor for him. Then the case was worked up so that, on paper at least, his conviction seemed an absolute certainty. His

The Known Thief's Expense Account

lawyer finally admitted to him that he was afraid
he could not save him. "The jury will railroad
you on general principles, in spite of the evidence," he said, "because you're known to be
a hard case; and my advice to you is to slope
and forfeit your bail, unless you want to enter
into negotiations with the district attorney's
office."

"Let's enter into negotiations," said Willson;
"I want to be able to come back to this town."

The negotiations resulted in Willson's adding
$5,000 to the $8,000 cash bail, and the indictment against him was quashed. The $13,000
was divided, so it is said, entirely among detectives and lawyers. Willson eventually re-
couped himself out of the winnings of the bank
job which he had contemplated when he sur-
rendered himself to the authorities. The rumor
is that he has since reformed and is no longer
to be found in gun circles. The last heard of
him by the Under World he was singing gospel
hymns at open-air revival meetings in the far
West in the interests of an attractive woman
evangelist, who considers him her main convert.

A natural query in connection with the estimates given in this chapter of the expense of a
criminal life is: Why do so many men go into
it? If it costs so much to be a thief, what is
the use of taking up with the profession? I

The World of Graft

cannot better answer these questions than by quoting an old retired "professional" to whom I put practically the same queries. He had told me with considerable detail how expensive it is "to run with guns," and how little a man has after a lifetime spent in their company; and I asked him point-blank why it was that men of his stamp could not see beforehand what failures they were bound to make of themselves.

"They can't see beforehand," he replied, repeating my words, "because they start out as failures. The average gun in this country begins life with about as much chance of getting on honestly as that dirty little bootblack over there on the corner. He's usually born in some city where he has to get out and hustle before he's even in his teens. Hustling in a big city for a kid means picking up his living where he can. Some shine shoes, some sell papers, and others become errand-boys. Not one out of ten thousand ever expects to amount to anything, or knows how to. They have very little education practically no friends, and only the money that they earn, and if they remain honest they can never possibly make more than a bare living. If they graft occasionally, on the other hand, they can blow themselves every now and then, and have their regular wages besides. If they're caught grafting they think that their life

The Known Thief's Expense Account

won't be any worse in the stir than on the street, and in winter not so bad perhaps. In time, some see that they can make a great deal more grafting than they can shining shoes and selling papers, and they prowl around for chances. They get pinched once in a while, and have to do their bits; but, as I said, life in the stir doesn't seem so bad to them, and they go grafting again when they're turned loose. At the end of a lifetime the most of them are just about where they were when they started out as kids, but they would probably have remained just as stationary, as far as getting on is concerned, if they'd tried to live on the level. They can't see ahead in the way that you mean, because they have everything to win and nothing to lose in making the experiment, and if they fail they're no worse off than they would have been had they not tried. In other words, they're all practically failures from the time that they're born till they die, and at the wind-up are about as happy as at the start. I'm just as poor to-day as I was when I began, and about as contented. It's cost me nothing to play the game, because I played it with O. P. M. (other people's money). Personally, I'm even with the game. I've been shut up a number of years, it's true, but I didn't mind them as much as you would; I took them as part of the spiel. If I had my life to live

[169]

over again, and couldn't start out any better than I did this time, I think I should go in for grafting again. It doesn't pay, and I know it doesn't, *but it's the one profession that as a ragamuffin I've got a fighting chance to win out in, and it amuses me to try my luck.*

"That's my explanation of why so many men are professional guns in spite of the costs. It is simply a matter of being a professional day-laborer, with the poorhouse staring you and your family in the face, and a professional thief, with the doors of the stir yawning for you. Personally, I think there's more amusement in looking at the doors of the stir."

The Tax-Payer's Bill

THE known and the unknown criminals in the United States constitute the most expensive luxury that the American people permit themselves. Our national liquor bill, large as it seems, is in my opinion a mere bagatelle compared with the expense which the big and little thieves cost us."

The foregoing statement was made to me by the late Austin Bidwell a few years after his release from his English prison. We had been talking about the relative merits of the English and American penological systems, and Bidwell was moved to criticise what he called our " spendthrift treatment " of offenders. He was such an authority in matters of this character—at least he made that impression on me—that I did not attempt to question the truthfulness of the remark, and merely noted it down in my memorandum-book. It comes back to me now in connection with my own findings of recent date, and I am constrained to repeat it here by way of introduction to what others have to say on the same subject.

The bill which the tax-payer has to pay on account of crime and its practitioners is levied

The World of Graft

partly by the criminal and partly by the officials who hunt him down, judge him, and watch him during his imprisonment. An appreciable sum also finds its way into the hands of political rings and bosses. The money which the criminal collects personally is the direct tax which his class imposes on the public, and the cost of trying, finding, and punishing him, the indirect. The amount of the direct tax in a year depends entirely on the luck that criminals have. If " business " is brisk, and there is a good deal " doing," the public is naturally mulcted much more than during lean years, when " touches " are few and far between; but year in and year out, millions of dollars are realized by our professional thieves, and to their winnings must be added the plunder of the occasional pilferers, as well as that of the " unmugged " offenders who steal only when there is a big sum to be landed and the chances of detection are slight. I asked a number of men for estimates of the probable total winnings of the professional criminals in a year, but they all gave me different answers. One man went as high as $50,000,000 in his guess, and another as low as $10,000,000. As none of my informants was sure of the number of " professionals " who are active, it was impossible for any of them to calculate nicely. They all had their own notions of the number

The Tax-Payer's Bill

of men who were entitled to be called "first-class" grafters, but they frankly admitted that it would be unfair to confine their estimates of the yearly plunder of the so-called "professionals" merely to those men whom they personally rated as such. I found also that the figures given me depended a good deal on the kind of "professional" meant. An old "bank" man was so disgusted with the present condition of his own particular branch of business that he declared there was hardly a living in it any longer. A New York pickpocket, on the other hand, was of the opinion that "things were just about as lively" in his branch as they had ever been, and he ventured the assertion that his class alone mulcted the public to the tune of $15,-000,000 every year. He was very enthusiastic about a recent "touch" of his own, and this may account in some measure for the large figure he mentioned; but I have heard other men, who were temporarily down on their luck, give estimates that were considerably higher.

An ex-"porch-climber," who is now a tramp, and claims that he can consequently look at the whole matter impartially—that it is immaterial to him how much the guns take in and the public gives out—spent an hour with me trying to formulate a statement of the yearly income of the entire class of "professionals," big and little, and I give here the pith of what he had to say, warning the reader, however, to remember that the tramp, like my other informants, could only make guesses.

"Countin' all kinds," he explained, "there's easily 1,000 A Number One guys in the country, ain't there? Course there's some that 'ud tell you that there's 10,000, but I'm goin' it easy. Now, an A Number One guy goes out for big money or none at all, don't he? You can't get him interested 'less there's a thousand or two in the job, an' he calls the year a bad one when the jobs don't come pretty frequently. Course he's with a mob most the time, an' the plunks has to be whacked up, but let's say, for the sake o' chewin' the rag, that the mob's made up o' five men an' they make ten touches in a year at a couple o' thousand per. Course the next year they may be all sloughed up, but when a first-class mob's loose 't ain't doin' anything wonderful to cop out $20,000 in a year. Now, I said that there was a thousand first-class guys in the country, didn't I? Split 'em up into mobs o' five, an' grantin' that they're all loose, they ought to take in in twelve months, accordin' to my $20,000 figurin', four million plunks, oughtn't they? Course, I know that the big guys cop out a lot more 'n that, but I'm just tryin' to figure out things so 's 't you can get a basis to

The Tax-Payer's Bill

sit on. Now, let's open up the throttle a little, an' chew the rag 'bout the other guys that's in the business but ain't real first class. The devil himself don't know how many thousands o' them there is, but not to hit the pipe too hard an' get to dreamin', let's say that there's 5,000. There may be 50,000, but you an' me can't prove it. They're all second class, ain't they? — some worse 'n that. Well, I used to be a second-class Johnny myself, so I can give you some straight goods. When I was in luck for six months— it never lasted much longer 'n that—I use to take in from $1,200 to $2,000. There was times when I didn't see the color o' five hundred, but I'm shoutin' 'bout the days when the coin came easy. Well, let's get an av'rige, an' call it $1,500 a year for the second-class guns, an' let's say that there's 3,000 o' them. That 'ud make $4,500,000 for the push, wouldn't it? The other two thousand o' the five we'll call pick-me-up guys, hobo guns, an' so forth. I'm livin' with the 'boes myself now, an' can tell you 'bout what those that steals gets. They're nearly all swag Johnnies; they rob cars an' houses an' sell the stuff they find. Five hunderd per 'll cover all that any of 'em takes in—easy. Multiply that by 2,000 an' you got a million plunks, ain't you? Now, add up your $1,000,000, $4,500,000, an' $4,000,000, an' you got $9,500,000. That stands

The World of Graft

for cash that the 6,000 feels an' hands around. It ain't all that the pub's lost in a year, 'cause a lot o' stuff that's swiped has to be sold at a sacrifice, as the Sheenies say, but on the basis 't we're sittin', it represents what the 6,000 guns puts in their pockets. Now, I know an' you know, 'f you've rubbered around at all, that $9,500,000 a year won't cover what the guns o' this country cops out, an' we both know, too, that there's more 'n 6,000 of 'em; but I just wanted to show you what the figures 'ud look like when they're kept real small. If you want my best guess 'bout the real figures—mind you, we ain't been doin' much guessin' so far—why, I can loosen up my imagination enough to say that the pub in this glorious country o' yours an' mine loses in a year, when all the guns are graftin', anywhere from $20,000,000 to $35,000,-000, an' those millions stands for cash that the boys handles after they've sold their swags an' made their get-aways. Tack on the sacrifices they have to make when sellin' the swag to the fences, an' the figures 'ud go up higher, so far as the pub's concerned—perhaps double. I'm only shoutin' 'bout the dough that the guns get their fists on. If it's more 'n what I say, then I'm a poor guesser, but I don't see any more, an' I guess the guns don't either."

From the point of view of the Under World

The Tax-Payer's Bill

the plunder which the unknown thief realizes in his raids is as much a direct tax on the public as is that of the known, and it must consequently be included in the calculation of the total receipts of the thieving class. It seems rather harsh to the Upper World to call a man a criminal who is merely unscrupulous in business or reckless in the management of public funds, but the Under World makes no distinction between him and the pickpocket so long as he profits and the public loses by his illegal transactions. How great his plunderings are is as difficult to determine as it was in the case of the regular " professionals; " even more so, because if he holds a position of trust he is able to cover up his thefts for a number of years, and the public does not know that it is being mulcted. A cashier of a bank, for instance, has been known to pilfer from his employers for a decade, and longer, without being even suspected, and no one knew except himself how much he was stealing until the whole story came out. For this reason, and also because a number of thefts by Upper World offenders are never brought to light—thanks to the " pull " which the offenders have—estimates of the relative amount stolen by the " unmugged " thieves are necessarily wild and untrustworthy. The Under World believes to a man that this " unmugged " graft exceeds by many millions the plunder won by the " profession," and as a general rule I believe this to be the case—a cashier of a bank, if he is dishonest, obviously has a better opportunity of making a large " haul " than has the " peter-man " who meditates an attempt upon that bank from the outside—but it is idle to try to figure out the amount of the excess. Several men that I met gave me long statements, statistical and otherwise, which were intended to show how much more the Upper World steals from the public than the men who are known to make a profession of stealing, but they were so obviously mere guesses that it is not worth while to restate them here. Suffice it to say that the average known thief is convinced that the unknown thieves make " get-aways " with plunder in a year that will run anywhere from fifty to a hundred million dollars in excess of the total winning of the known thief's class.

The story of the indirect tax which the criminals of this country impose on the public can only be outlined in this chapter because it would take a book merely to give the statistical part of it, but it is a tale that ought to be told in full to bring home to the reader the immensity of the tax and the nonsensical way in which much of it is expended. All that can be attempted here, however, is to indicate roughly what it

The Tax-Payer's Bill

costs the public to police the Under World, to try it in court, take care of it in prison, and settle some of the bills of the league between the Powers that Rule and the Powers that Prey. It is the professional thief's opinion that it costs the public a great deal more to apprehend, convict, and punish an unknown thief of the Upper World than a known thief of the Under, and a statement in regard to the relative expense in each case would be necessary in a complete rendering of the bill; but it is impossible to make a satisfactory statement of this kind at present, and furthermore it is for the Under World rather than the Upper—theoretically at least—that our police, courts, and punitive institutions are intended.

In the criminal's opinion the cost of policing the Under World is the biggest indirect tax that the public has to pay on his account. If there were no " professionals," and the thieving class was composed only of occasional offenders, he believes that the bill which the tax-payer now has to pay for police purposes could be reduced fully one-half. Take New York City, by way of example. It costs the citizens something like $10,000,000 to pay for the present " protection " which the city is supposed to have. Admitting, for the sake of argument, that this sum is necessary under the existing circumstances to pro-

The World of Graft

vide for adequate police supervision—the Under World says that it is altogether too much—my informants declare that $5,000,000 would suffice if the guns now located in New York and passing in and out every day were excluded from residence in the city. The same statement is said to hold good of Chicago, as well as of several other large cities. Besides the municipal police, there are also private detective organizations which the public makes use of in ferreting out crime, and which demand their share of the tax which the defence against the criminal class makes necessary. Some remarks of a Bostonian, whom I interviewed in regard to the matter of police expense, will throw light on these institutions.

" Some of 'em bleed the pub," he said, " worse than any municipal police force in the country, and I can prove it to you right out of my own experience. Some years ago a Western guy and I had a business deal on up in Maine. It was a sort of ' Franklin Syndicate' kind of affair, except that we didn't promise such a big per cent. Things went along smooth as oil for about three months, and we were takin' in the coin by the handful—that is for Maine. The old State ain't got much except woods, you know. At the end of the three months the suckers began to get leary, and they clubbed to-

The Tax-Payer's Bill

gether and put some private fly-cops on to us. Well, the cops saw that they was dealin' with a lot o' Rubes, and took their time. We hung out for about six weeks longer and then vamoosed, and the fly-cops were sent after us. We stood trial and were acquitted—our lawyer fixed the thing up. The Rubes lost what they'd paid us besides eighteen hundred plunks that the detective agency made them cough up. I saw the bill from the agency 'cause the Rubes wanted us to pay it. The expense charges alone were $1,100. That's where the swindle comes in and where the pub gets it in the neck. The agency asks, say, $10 a day and expenses. The fly-cop gets $20 or $25 a week from the agency and so much for expenses. He grafts off the man that's payin' the agency, by putting in a big bill for railroad tickets, hotels, and so forth. The agency stands for the bill, and the fly-cop pockets the difference between what he has actually spent and what he says that he has. I ain't knockin' against the fly-cop—he's got to graft to live— but you see, don't you, how the pub has to cough up? If you add up all that the private agencies cost the pub, together with the municipal police forces—and just on account o' guns, mind you—you'll get a bigger sum than the pub has any idea of. I got to figuring it up one day, a few years ago, when I was doin' solitary

[181]

The World of Graft

down in Philadelphia. You know how it is when you're doin' solitary—you get to thinkin' about all kinds o' things, and I got to addin' and subtractin' about what it costs this country to police it. I don't remember the particular items any more, but I got a total, countin' the private detective agencies, railroad coppers, and Secret Service people, somewhere about $125,000,000 a year, and I'd reckoned just as closely as I knew how. A fellow ought to be able to find out just how much it is if he could get at the records of all the different forces, but I'll bet you that if the real figures ever comes out you'll see that mine was under rather than over the mark."

"Do you think that the private detective agencies are a necessity in policing the country?"

"If the municipal police forces were on the level, no. That is, for takin' care of guns. Course you can't expect a municipal force to help you get a divorce, and that's where a private detective agency always gets in its graft; but that ain't police work. The reason that the agencies have so much to do is because the town coppers can't be relied on, or are too lazy to get down to business. Take the Pinkertons. If you were a gun and had robbed my bank, I'd rather put the case in their hands than in the hands o' the Boston police, say, *because it's their business to find you,* and they're goin' to do it if

The Tax-Payer's Bill

huntin' for you 'll accomplish it. The Pinkertons hire men for what they can do, and not on account o' political pull or because they're Irishmen or niggers, and that's the reason they get such a lot of business."

"Then the present corruption among our municipal police is favorable to the interests of the private agencies?"

"Most certainly it is. You won't find a proprietor of a private agency that's sighin' for reform of the police outside of a dime museum, and I don't think you can find any there."

This same man gave me as interesting an account as any, of the probable cost of our courts in connection with the Under World. Apropos of his estimate of the cost of the police, I asked him whether he had ever calculated the expense to the tax-payer of trying the Under World after the police had locked it up, and he gave me some facts out of his own personal experience by way of illustration.

"I've been railroaded (convicted, sentenced, and punished) four times since I've been on the turf," he said, "and I've been pinched, tried, and let loose easily seven. That ain't much of a record compared with some that I could tell you about, but it 'll do for an average. Now, let's take the first time that I was railroaded. It was for a swindlin' job in Connecticut, and

[183]

my defence was an alibi. I tried to prove, and
I subpœnaed eighty-five witnesses to help me
prove, that I was in Massachusetts when the deal
that I was charged with was pulled off. I was
guilty all right enough, and I told my lawyers
so, but I was goin' to make the prosecution
convince the jury o' the fact. I was like all
guns, and wanted the thing done right; see?
Well, sir, the thing dragged along for over two
months before I was even brought to trial—the
prosecution wanted to collect evidence, and
spent hundreds of dollars doin' it. Meanwhile
I was bein' supported in the jail at the expense
of the county. The trial lasted nearly ten days.
The lawyers fought like bull-dogs, and kept
draggin' the thing along till nearly every man
on the jury got sick. I had over fifty witnesses
on my side that came, and the prosecution had
nearly as many. I'd 'a' subpœnaed the whole
bloomin' State if I could, 'cause when I see 't
I'm goin' to get it in the neck anyhow I like to
make just as much trouble as I can. Well, they
convicted me at last and I got a two-spot; but
what do you think it cost the State to railroad
me? Thirty-seven hundred dollars and ninety-
five cents, and I was only supposed to have
made $1,600 out of my swindle! Some o' the
tax-payers said that I ought to have been hung
for that amount of money, and they was right,
too.

The Tax-Payer's Bill

" Now, take one of the times that they had to turn me loose. I use to live over in western New York some years ago, and I got a lot of the farmers in my neighborhood interested in a co-operative cheese factory. It was a deal 't I'd thought about a lot, and the farmers bit like suckers. I was manager of the thing an' took in all the dough. Well, there was to be a general meetin' one day, an' I was to make a statement about the affairs o' the association. I'd salted away about $2,000 in cash that was due to go to the bank in a neighborin' town as soon as the meetin' was over. The night before the meetin' I got a pal to rob my house; he took an overcoat an' a pair o' rubbers—it was a rainy night—an' that was all. The next mornin' I hollered 't I'd been touched for the two thousand, an' told the farmers so at the meeting. They shouted and bellered, an' in about a week had me arrested. The trial lasted two weeks, an' both sides subpœnaed dozens o' witnesses. My witnesses said that I had a good character, an' the farmers said 't I hadn't. Well, the thing fiddled along until the day before the prosecutor was goin' to make his speech, when the farmers said they'd be glad to settle with me for twenty-five cents on the dollar. I heard afterward that the prosecutor told them that they could never convict me. He took up the case 'cause he

wanted them to vote for him for county treas-
urer or somethin' else. I settled with 'em, an'
the county paid the bill o' the trial. It came
to $1,400.

"I could go on an' give you some more ex-
amples, but they're all about alike; the State
paid the bills whether I was railroaded or not.
Altogether the different trials I've had must 'a'
cost the pub $10,000, an' I'm only one out o'
thousands. For the sake o' figurin', let's say
that there's 25,000 guns in the country. Some
are first class, an' some ain't got no class at all,
but they're all grafters. Let's say also that it
costs the tax-payer $2,000 apiece to try 'em for
the various jobs that they do before they die.
That makes $50,000,000 for the whole push,
don't it? Fifty million plunks to try one generation o' guns! It's my opinion that the pub
'ud consider itself lucky if it got off with a hundred million. There's no better place in the
world for bills to get big than in a court-room,
and if you ever get a grudge against the pub
or your home State, just do some big job, make
'em try you on the level, an' then drag the thing
out. You'll work your grouch off sure if your
lawyers understand their business, take my tip
for that. It's the easiest and best way there is
o' gettin' even with the world."

The expense of housing and feeding the Un-

The Tax-Payer's Bill

der World in our prisons, after it has been caught, tried, and convicted need not be considered in detail here, because it is pretty well known in each State what the local lock-ups, jails, reformatories, workhouses, and penitentiaries cost; but it must be remembered that in every community where these institutions are found they constitute a part of the indirect tax of which the professional criminal is one of the main causes. What was said about the professional offender in connection with the police may be repeated here in connection with our prisons—the amount which they now cost might be very appreciably reduced if the habitual law-breaker could be eliminated from the problem which they are supposed to help solve. One of the "burning" questions of the day in Under World circles is whether the prisoners in our penitentiaries shall be furnished with work or not, and I have listened to a number of conversations in regard to this subject. It is usually discussed entirely from the point of view of the prisoner, who, it is contended, must have something to occupy his mind while in durance if he is to be reformed; but the economic side of the argument is also frequently taken up, and there are those who declare that the tax-payer is silly in not making the prisoner help support himself. An old tramp, who claimed to be an ex-

The World of Graft

gun, said to me in Pennsylvania: "I've been shut up nearly eighteen years of my life, and ten of them in prisons where there was work for only a few of the prisoners. In other words, the tax-payer has handed out hard cash most of this time just to keep me alive, and yet when I was turned loose it was my business to relieve him of some more cash on my own account. Now, what kind of sense do you call that? I don't see any sense in it at all. The workin'man says that he won't compete with me in the market because I have to work for nothing. But if I don't work, hasn't he got to go down deeper in his pocket than if I did? Ain't that straight? I tell you what's the matter with some of our workin'men — they got lightnin'-rods in their headpieces. They let some walkin' delegate chew the rag to 'em till they're all tied up with words, and then they go it blind. I'm nothin' but an old 'bo so far as position goes, but I can beat the workin'man figurin' out this prison-labor business just the same; and if I was runnin' a prison I'd make the prisoners in it work their ten hours every day. It would do them good and save the tax-payer money."

Reference has been made to some of the expenses due to the league between the Powers that Rule and the Powers that Prey as also constituting a part of the indirect tax under con-

The Tax-Payer's Bill

sideration. A glance at the situation in New York City will make this clear. The league could not exist in New York without the tacit consent of the ruling political bosses, and the bosses, as was stated in the chapter on New York, could not remain in power if they refused the Under World—I use the expression now in its broadest sense—the chance to live, which means to graft. The bosses need the Under World—its votes and good-will—in order to retain their hold of the municipal offices. Any expenses that may accrue from these direct transactions between the two Powers are paid by the contracting parties in ways satisfactory to both, and the public is not mulcted, except when " touched " directly by the pickpocket or burglar. The indirect tax comes in when the public has to pay the bill presented by the political organization which happens to be running the city. The Under World settles this account only in part in the shape of hush-money and bribes; the big items are paid by the tax-payer, and they are made big because the Powers that Rule demand such immense sums to run the city on the " league " basis. It is the universal opinion of all the men that I talked with, that New York could be managed on an honest basis at least a third more cheaply than it is now with the league in force. If this be true, then the indirect tax which the league involves is obviously one of the heaviest which the dwellers in cities have to pay. Much of it, no doubt, like the contributions of the Under World to the bosses, is never recorded in the tax-books or collected through official channels, but it is handed over as punctually—even more so in many cases—as is the tax on property.

PART V

RECOMMENDATIONS OF
CERTAIN DEAD ONES

What the Dead Ones Say Should be Done

THE Dead Ones are the inhabitants of the Under World who have " squared it "— given up professional thieving and begun something else. Some become tramps, perhaps the majority; others develop into small gamblers, billiard markers, and " lighthouses " (look-outs) for " cribs " (gambling joints); while still others seek shelter as detectives in municipal and private police organizations. But they are all " dead." They have all gone under in the struggle to make names and fortunes in the aristocracy of the World of Graft. They are the wrecks and débris left by the wayside, while their younger and more energetic companions trudge on. Some have dropped out of the ranks on account of the " shivers "—the palsy that comes over certain criminals; others have lost heart from repeated defeats and punishments, and prefer to give up their ambition rather than go utterly to pieces like their palsied brethren; and there are hundreds who have retreated to Hoboland by choice, convinced that their endowment of criminal wit is not sufficient to allow them to compete with their more talented and persevering pals. Collected into institutions and asylums, they would present quite as pitiful a sight as do the weak and maimed in the retreats which society builds for the invalid. The active criminal, on viewing an old companion stricken down with the shivers, has the same mingled feeling of pity and revulsion that comes over us all when we visit a friend in the insane ward of one of our sanitariums. While at work and in the heat of the chase for plunder the criminal is one of the hardest and most obtuse human beings in existence; the same may be said of a number of business men; but when off duty, and free to exercise the gentleness and charity with which he is almost always endowed in some measure, he has moments of friendly feeling toward his fellow-man which in sincerity the Upper World cannot surpass. If he could only prolong these moments into days and weeks, and were less of a money-spender and more of a saver, it is no fanciful statement to say that the Under World would have long since provided poorhouses and hospitals of its own, and the Dead Ones would not be the pathetic wanderers that they are to-day. As has been explained, however, it is an inexorable law among outcasts that money is to be scat-

What the Dead Ones Say

tered and not hoarded, and so the old and worn-out among them have no charity fund on which to draw. When they die, society buries them if their own world has forgotten to do it, and they pick their way on to the end, assured at least of a berth in the " underground hang-out."

My reason for letting these men tell what ought to be done to clean up the criminal situation in our cities is that they have played the game to a finish and can explain how and why they failed to win out, and how others can be similarly discouraged. They are in a position, which the active criminal is not, to look at the whole matter retrospectively as well as prospectively, and they are also willing talkers and critics. The active criminal does not absolutely refuse to give his opinion about possible reforms and changes, but to do so does not interest him as it does the Dead One. The latter has nothing to lose or gain by what he says, and he speaks his mind freely, without fear of his own world or the one upon which he used to prey. What he reports is often trite and old, but every now and then his eyes brighten with intelligence, his face takes on the hard look of former days when every man's hand was raised against him, and he talks about the World of Graft like one inspired. It is then that one must ask him for advice, and I have collected into this last chap-

[195]

The World of Graft

ter some of the suggestions he made during the
conversations I had with him on my recent tour
of investigation. As will be seen by the reader
who is interested enough to go through them
to the end, they all presuppose an immense
amount of hard work and a determination on
the part of the public to have a satisfactory defence against crime, no matter what it costs,
but I see no reason why this makes them any
the less valuable. Crime is never going to be
stopped and the police are never going to be
made honest and efficient by magic. The thief
will continue to steal as long as the pain of the
punishment meted out to him does not exceed
the joy which his plunder brings him, and the
police will continue to graft until public sentiment and good citizenship make it impossible.
The thief's suggestions as to how his profession can be made unprofitable, and as to the
best means of keeping the police under control, can hardly be formulated into a general
scheme of reform which can be applied indis-
criminately, and I have made no attempt to draw
conclusions from them or to prognosticate what
would probably happen if they were acted upon.
My aim is merely to report verbatim what the
Under World, as represented by its Dead Ones,
has to say about certain things which everybody
agrees ought to be changed and can be changed

[196]

if there is a will to do it, but which our municipal governments find it very difficult to cope with.

One of the most interesting critics of the police that I met was a Dead One who lives in Chicago. He left the profession early enough to gather himself together for a new start in life, and he lives at present quite comfortably, for a man of his class, in a modest little West Side home. We fell to talking one day about the police and the criminals of Chicago, and I asked him how he would go about it to clean up the city—to make the police live " on the level " and the criminals stop their thieving. He hesitated a moment before replying, but it was not on account of unwillingness to express his opinion, as he finally explained.

" That's a big question, neighbor," he said. " O' course I can tell you what I think and what I'd do 'f I was runnin' things at the Front Office, but I might get left after all. It's a mighty hard proposition, this keepin' the police straight, an' I ain't sure that I'd succeed in doin' it 'f I had all the power that the city can give me. What I'd try to do is what any man who was on the level and thought he had the pub behind him would make a stab at; so what I tell you 'll hold good for York as well as it will for Chi. I know Chi better 'n I do York, but as far as what I'd

The World of Graft

do is concerned I might just as well exper'ment with York as this berg here. Some people thinks that because a man's been a gun he ought to know just how guns can be discouraged, but he can no more prescribe the right med'cine for *ev'ry* gun than he can tell how *ev'ry* town can get a decent police force. I can tell you how *I* was discouraged and how *I'd* go to work to discourage others, just as I can tell you what *I'd* try for 'f I was chief o' police in Chi, but you'll prob'ly meet somebody else to-morrow who'll tell you something quite differ'nt.

"The main trouble with the police o' this country is that they're in politics. That ain't anythin' new, an' I know it, but you want to hear what a Dead One has to say, an' I'm givin' it to you. If I had my way, the police o' the United States 'ud be put under the national government the way the army is, an' ev'ry State 'ud have an inspector sent out from Washington."

"Don't you think that such a plan would merely increase the possibilities of crooked work?"

"Course it would if the people didn't kick; I'm goin' on the basis that the citizens want a square police and are willin' to pay for it. Mind you, I don't believe that they really do want a square police force, otherwise they'd get rid of

What the Dead Ones Say

the crooked coppers. No man livin' can be crooked long in a community where the pub is stuck on havin' things on the level. I'm as sure o' that as I am that you an' me is chewin' the rag now. An' if I was made chief here to-morrow I'd ask the people straight out exactly what they wanted, an' I'd give 'em exactly what they asked for, or t'row up the posish. The prob'bility is that the big push here in Chi 'ud tell me not to go the goody-goody racket too strong, an' so I'd have to let some o' the boys graft. If some o' the boys grafted, others 'ud want to, an' 't wouldn't be long 'fore things 'ud be as bad as ever. You can't play with graftin' any more 'n you can with dynamite. When I first started out on the road I only intended to steal a little, I didn't mean to be a perfeshnul. It's the little stealin's that make a man want the big ones, an' that's how I got into the peter business. It's the same thing with the coppers. You've got to have 'em absolutely on the level, an' the pub has got to be with you, or they'll graft right under your very nose.

"I was readin' an article 'bout that the other day that some guy wrote for one o' the maga-zines. He was a reformer an' a goody-goody, I guess, besides, but he put the facts down for fair. I don't remember his words, but what he said was somethin' like this: ' Go the whole hog

[199]

The World of Graft

or none at all.' (He was writin' 'bout munic'pul politics.) ' Go the whole bloomin' hog,' he says, ' an' let the pub see that you're goin' to fight it out on that basis if it takes all winter, as Grant said. If you've got anythin' good in your reformin' scheme it'll win out in the end.'

" That's what I say about the police, an' I'm nothin' but an old ex-gun, an' couldn't write an article for the magazines to save my headpiece. Get the people interested in wantin' coppers that won't graft, an' then fire ev'ry bloomin' one that does. That's the only way that you'll ever get Chi or York or any other berg cleaned up, an' if you live to be a hunderd you won't discover anythin' else that's better. I know it 'cause I've watched the business hard for over thirty years, an' can tell what works an' what doesn't. The reason 't I want the police under the national government is that the pub can't change its mind so quick as it can now with the police run by the cities. It 'ud have to take four years o' the thing anyhow, an' a hell of a lot can be done by the police in that time if they're on the level. W'y, I'd be willin' to guarantee to corral ev'ry good gun in the country in four years 'f I was chief o' such a force. With the national government behind him, a wise copper could sweep this country absolutely clean o' perfeshnuls."

What the Dead Ones Say

"Why can't the Secret Service Department at Washington do it, then?" I asked.

"In the first place because it hasn't got a big enough force, and in the second because it only keeps track o' guns that graft off the government. But I can tell you that when I used to be on the turf there was nobody 't I hated worse to have on my track, exceptin' the Big Man, than a Secret Service guy, an' just because 't I knew 't he had the government behind him. I used to touch up P. O. boxes now an' then, an' I made one or two nice get-aways, but it's the leariest work 't I ever done. For weeks after I'd made that kind of a touch I'd worry about bein' copped out. A gun, you know, is a superstitious old fool, an' I use to think sometimes when I was worryin' that the government had nothin' but eyes. It couldn't 'a' seemed any more terrible to me 'f I'd thought 't was the Almighty himself. Once, I remember, after I'd done a government job, I had a dream that the Almighty was after me for sure. They say 't if a fellow don't wake up out o' them kind o' dreams the Almighty actually does get him, but I woke up, an' I was mighty glad 't I did, too. You're all in a perspiration when you dream ghost stories like that."

"Do many guns dream them?"

"Oh, I don't know; not many, I guess; but

[201]

The World of Graft

you see what I'm drivin' at, don't you? I say that the police have got to be so strong and straight that a gun thinks o' home an' mother right away the minute he knows they're after him. There's guns that get scared silly when they hear that the Big Man's after 'em, an' my idea is that you got to put the police under the government before they'll stop graftin' an' learn how to frighten guns. That's what I'd do anyhow if I was the high monkey-monk in this country. Course I could go on an' tell you how I'd pick out my men, but that's a small matter. The big thing is to get the coppers under the right system, an' I don't believe you'll ever be able to do it lettin' the towns run their own police forces."

There were others who favored the municipal management of the police with state supervision. One man, for instance, believed that the towns could be relied on to superintend their own police successfully, if they knew that an inspector was likely to appear at any moment from the governor of the State with full power to overhaul the different police organizations. He seemed to have in mind an official somewhat similar to the " revisor " of Russia whom Gogol made the subject of his comedy. The revisor is sent by the Czar unannounced to a town about which he wants a report, and all the officials are under him while he is conducting his investigations. The Dead One in question was convinced that such a man, who might be called a general superintendent of police, would be a sufficient check on the various police forces to secure their good behavior.

Still another Dead One advocated the policing of our cities by private detective organizations, more or less similar to the Pinkerton Detective Agency. This suggestion has been referred to in another chapter, and it may be repeated here that there is no doubt in the average criminal's mind that such an arrangement would be much cheaper than the present system of municipal police management, but among the Dead Ones it was not so popular as a remedy for existing conditions as the plan of governmental control. Next in favor to the national supervision of the police seemed to be the revisor suggestion. An old New York offender was so enamoured of the latter scheme that he declared that New York City would be a " closed town " inside of six months if there was a final authority at Albany who rigidly inspected the police organizations of the State.

" Of course he's got to be on the level," he added, " or the thing wouldn't work. But you put an honest man in such a position, give him the right to discharge men, chiefs included, and let

[203]

no one be over him whom the discharged coppers can appeal to, and the flatties and elbows o' this old town 'ud be so polite and good that they could go to heaven any day. I know 'em down to the ground. All that they need is somebody to curl 'em up with a red-hot poker, and then they're as obedient as kids."

Concerning the general administration of cities, there was not much that has not already been touched upon in the previous chapters that the Dead Ones had to contribute, but they discuss this subject as freely as they talk about the police. The situation in New York City seemed to interest them most, and they all had something to say about the way the " Hoosiers up State try to run the town." Although a number of them were in favor of state management of the police on the lines laid down, they were all against having the legislature at Albany tell the city how it should live, and their criticisms of the present condition of things were aimed mainly at this abuse of power, as they consider it.

" I ain't any more stuck on Tammany Hall than the reformers are when it comes to having a thing done right," said one man, " but I don't want those yaps up at Albany runnin' things either. What do they know about how a big city like this should be managed? All that they know is how to milk cows, make cheese, and

What the Dead Ones Say

sit around the cook-stove in winter. And when they do come to town they cut up worse than the people who live here. I've seen 'em up in the Tenderloin, an' can pick 'em out ev'ry time just from the way they act. They swagger around as if they owned the town, and when they get touched they holler like stuck pigs. I know how they holler 'cause I've touched 'em myself.

"I'll never forget one guy that come down from Albany durin' Cleveland's first campaign for pres'dent. He had a few bowls in him already when he got here — those up-state guys like their booze, if they are farmers—an' he put a dozen more under his belt 'fore he'd even got started up-town. I first got sight of him in Broadway, and I followed him about a bit to see what kind of a roll he had. He was handin' out tens and twenties as if they was nickels. He thought he was French, an' kept shoutin', 'Toola maund,' in ev'ry joint he went into; he wanted to make out 't he was eddicated. I trailed him along till he struck the up-town district, an' then I put a pal next to him. He touched him for his roll an' his thimble,* an' the next mornin' there was hollerin' from the Battery to 110th Street. Didn't do no good though, an' he had to go home. I saw him just before he left. He was standin' with one of his

* Watch.

[205]

political friends on the dock where the Albany boat starts from. ' Jim,' he says to his friend, ' if God 'll forgive me this time, I'll never do it again.' He looked 's if he'd been eatin' poison ivy. His face was all mapped out in red blotches, an' his eyes was so bloodshot you could hardly see the green in 'em.

"Well, sir, that old Hoosier's been chewin' the rag about the corruption in York ever since, an' he's one o' the push that wants Albany to open her mouth wide ev'ry time there's anything to be done down here. He don't know how this town ought to be run any more 'n a kid does, an' yet you an' me has got to listen when he chews the rag. Now, that ain't the way a big berg like this ought to be managed, an' I know it ain't. Albany hasn't got any more right to mix in our troubles than London has, an' the town won't go right till it runs itself." I suggested that it made quite as much of a botch of things when running itself as when having to reckon with Albany.

"That may be, neighbor," the man continued, "but there's nobody but ourselves to blame when that happens, and you're gettin' things where they ought to be when you know that you can put yourself in the soup or keep out of it. The way things are now, you can't tell whether it's Albany or Tammany that's most to blame."

What the Dead Ones Say

There were also those who thought that the mayor of a city ought to be the supreme ruler —both active and " dead " guns, although very democratic in some things, seem to consider one-man power a panacea for nearly all governmental disturbances—and still others championed the cause of a secret organization of " regulators" who were to call the municipal officials to order when the latter were found neglecting their duties; but these suggestions were so contrary to American customs that I merely record them here without giving the explanations of how they would work which were tacked on to them. Indeed, there was so little that was practicable in what the Dead Ones had to say about how cities should be managed, except in connection with the police department, that it did not seem to me that much could be learned from them.

Their criticism of the American attitude toward crime, on the other hand, struck me as being something that the public might well ponder over, and I give here a conversation that I had with a very well educated man, who, although he has long since given up criminal work as his profession, has been unable to make anything more out of himself than a moderately successful hobo. He is frequently to be seen in City Hall Park, where he reads newspapers hour after hour, and holds conferences with his more

The World of Graft

intimate companions about the life that has passed, the present life, and the life to come. He is a pathetic example of the Dead Ones who have lost their grip in the "stir," but he can tell you, as few men can, how easy it is to become a criminal in the United States; and in quoting him, I am giving, I think, the consensus of opinion among men of his class in regard to the way crime is looked upon by the average American. We had our talk in a resort in Bleecker Street, where the tramp was not at home and had to speak in the midst of dancing, singing, and boisterous laughter; but he could not have stated his criticism any more calmly had we been riding in a box-car.

"Mind you," he said, after we had taken our seats, referring to a statement made in the street about the country being full of grafters, "I don't mean for an instant that everybody grafts or would if he could. I know as well as you that there are a great many good people in the world; but grafting is somehow or other in the air on this side of the water, and you find it in business as well as in politics. The business man is looking just as hard to make a pile as the professional gun is, and if it is his neighbor that he gets the best of, it makes no difference—business is business, and every man has got to take his chances. That's the spirit

What the Dead Ones Say

of things over here, no matter where you go, and some of the most successful men commercially are noted for having done some very tricky things. Now, the would-be gun, or the beginner in criminal life, is affected by this code of morals in about the same way that the would-be business man is; he begins to think out ways and means by which he can succeed. He wants to succeed quick; he hates work and loves excitement, and the gun's life attracts him. If he fails in his enterprises he is of course called a miserable criminal, but I can assure you that if he is successful for a while and makes some notoriously big strikes, there are hundreds of thousands of so-called respectable people who speak of him as a mighty smart fellow, and not as a thief. He is succeeding in making money quickly, and, as I say, a large part of the public overlooks his methods, and judges merely his performance.

"Take my own case. When I used to be on the turf I read time and again in the newspapers about how clever I was and how difficult it was to get ahead of me. That kind of talk has bolstered me up many a time when I was down on my luck, and I go and read even now in old newspaper files some of the paragraphs that used to be written about me. There was a time when I used to think that the public didn't care very

much whether I was a criminal or not, so long
as I got there, and did it cleverly. I felt more
or less like a dissipated actor who knows that
he does some vile things off the stage, but believes that they are excused on account of his
fine representations on the boards. Of course,
the time came when my nerve gave out, and
then everybody spoke of me merely as an old
burglar, but as long as I did my trick in a slick
way, and the American sense of smartness was
satisfied, I was ' that wizard with the jimmy, So-
and-So.'

"It's in many respects the same to-day as
it was when I was in the perfesh; the public
still applauds in secret, and sometimes in public—see how the Chicago newspapers comment
on the clever boldness with which some of the
hold-ups are done!—the fly work of guns. Naturally it's the plunder rather than the applause
that the guns are after, but the point I'm trying to make is that they think that the public
doesn't consider them as bad as they are, and
is prepared to admire the cleverness of their
work, if not its criminality. Such a conviction
is the same consolation to them as it was to me,
and encourages them in their careers. Consequently, I say that until the attitude of the
public in this country toward crime and criminals
changes and a theft is recognized as a theft,

What the Dead Ones Say

no matter by whom committed, it will be exceedingly difficult to reform professional guns. It took twenty-six years to peter me out, and I'm only discouraged as it is. If from the very start, on the other hand, I had been made to feel that the law was going to be administered conscientiously every time I was captured, and that the public utterly abhorred my conduct, I might have been petered out years before I was and with the conviction implanted in me that I had to take up honest work if I intended to live in this country. I think every man with my experience will tell you the same thing. They play with crime in the United States, and it is because the gun knows this that he is able to stay in the profession so many years."

A number of similar statements were made to me by other men whom I interviewed. Personally, I think that they misconstrue much that is said and written about them, and see compliments and applause where mere expression of wonderment is meant, but it is at least interesting to know that they think their performances are appreciated in the respectable world as well as in their own. Certainly there was a great deal too much romance thrown about Jesse James's personality, to take but one conspicuous instance of injudicious hero-worship on the part of a section of the public, and it

[211]

The World of Graft

is probably more or less similar adulation of smaller fry that my tramp acquaintance deplored.

To ask the criminal, even when he has become a Dead One, to offer suggestions whereby his profession may be made unprofitable, will doubtless strike the reader as a very strange proceeding, but to the Dead Ones with whom I talked it seemed quite as natural a phase of the matter as any of the others that I touched upon. The time comes in the life of an ex-gun when hope of ever re-entering the profession with success is so completely abandoned that he finds it a surcease of sorrow to persuade someone to listen to his stories and theories, and he does not hesitate to tell frankly how he was discouraged, and, at times, how he thinks others might be. His penological theories are often antiquated and in many instances cruel and barbaric, but he is not one of those who believe that the criminal is lacking in moral and mental aptitudes and consequently cannot be held responsible for his crimes. To him the professional thief is a man who, as a boy, was an occasional thief in order to have pocket money; as a young man, an understudy of some successful burglar, pickpocket, or " peter-man "; and as a mature person, a representative of a profession which has its place in the social order, or disorder, just as medicine and law have theirs. Stealing, in his opinion, is a business in which the accumulation of money, or rather the acquisition of it, has the same importance that it has in legitimate commerce; and there are those who succeed and fail just as there are those who win and lose in ordinary business enterprises. "We're all in this world to get money," a Dead One said to me in Philadelphia, "and I used to get mine my way, and my neighbors got theirs in a different way. All businesses are alike to me when it's money that I'm gunnin' for, and that's the reason that I call the professional thief a business man. He studies the market, makes investments, takes chances, and wins or loses, as he has planned well or poorly, and your merchant princes do the same."

Considered thus merely as a business man, the Dead Ones find it comparatively easy to suggest methods by which the professional criminal can be made to look upon thieving as an unprofitable enterprise. Some of their proposed methods naturally differ in detail—each man has his pet notion to advance—but all of their propositions culminate eventually in one — viz., punishment. The most passionate believer in the eternal damnation of lost souls that has ever existed had no greater faith in the efficacy of promised

The World of Graft

pain and suffering to frighten human beings into being righteous than has the Dead One when discussing the proper means to discourage business criminals. He believes in punishment and retribution as the devout religionist believes in his creed, and you may talk to him about the new penology and institutions such as the Elmira Reformatory, which seek a regeneration of offenders on more or less gentle lines, until you are utterly exhausted, and his last remark will be: " Give 'em the dark cell, if you can't scare 'em in the light one." For him it is simply a matter of convincing the thief that there is no money in grafting as a business, and to do this he declares that it is necessary, when you catch him, to make him suffer as he has never suffered before.

One of the last things my friend Sam— " The Man Who Has Squared It "—said to me, was: " I don't care what the reformers say or the wardens of penitentiaries experiment with; the only thing that 'll ever stop professional stealing is punishment. If I were runnin' a stir, and had the full say about the professional guns, I'd never let 'em go out on parole, I'd never let 'em be pardoned, an' I'd never let up on 'em while they was servin' out their bits. An' if I was a judge, an' a gun came up before me for

What the Dead Ones Say

sentence, I'd talk to him this way: 'You're a professional thief, you make your living by stealing other people's money. I want you to learn that that business don't pay, so I sentence you to the penitentiary to be punished just as hard as you can be and still keep alive. I give you only one year, because if you're punished right it's all you'll ever need.' If the first bit that I had to do had been made what I call hot as hell and twice as thirsty, I'd prob'ly never 'a' needed another, an' might have amounted to something to-day. Because it was easy, an' I could buy privileges when they wasn't given to me, I kept on graftin', an' I could prob'ly spend the rest o' my life in a stir an' feel at home. There's hunderds like me, an' we're still cumberin' the earth, as the educated people say, just because the people who was dealin' with us was too sentimental to give us what we deserved an' what would 'a' done us a lot o' good."

This is the testimony of nearly all the Dead Ones who have seen fit to talk with me about their own experience in prisons, and I may add that I have received similar statements from men who are still actively engaged in grafting. As a penological theory it does not fit in well with the present prevailing notions and practices— the professional criminal is treated in many of

our prisons quite as tenderly as is the first offender—but it is a contribution to the science
of penology from the very men for whom the
science exists, and for this reason, if for no other,
it seems to me to deserve very serious consideration.

PART VI

GLOSSARY

GLOSSARY

THE slang used by the crook is in many respects very similar to the ordinary slang heard in the street, but there are some words which would not be understood outside of Graftdom. The following collection of terms is not meant to be at all exhaustive; I have merely explained the meaning of the more obscure words used in the text.

B

BEEF, } to " squeal " or ELCH, } " split " on a pal.

BIG MAN, the Pinkerton Detective Agency.

BIT, a term in prison.

BOOK, pocketbook.

BUGHOUSE, crazy.

C

CALL THE TURN, give the name and record of a gun. When a detective identifies a criminal he is said to have called the turn on him.

COPPED OUT, arrested.

CRIB, gambling dive.

D

DEAD, out of touch with current events in the world of graft; the antithesis of " wise."

DIP, pickpocket. ON THE DIP, on a pocket-picking excursion. STALLING FOR THE DIP, assisting the " tool," or pickpocket, in arranging victims so that they can be successfully robbed.

E

ELBOW, detective.

F

FALL MONEY, funds saved by criminals to pay lawyers, secure cash bail, and to bribe officials.

FENCE, receiver of stolen property.

FLATTY, } uniformed police-FINGER, } man.

FLY-COP, detective.

FRONT OFFICE, police headquarters.

[219]

Glossary

G

GET - AWAY, successful retreat with plunder.

GOPHER-MEN, safe-blowers.

GUN, thief.

H

HOLLER, the plaint of the victim.

K

KNOCK, also means to "squeal."

L

LEATHER, pocket-book.

M

MOB, a collection of guns who work together. Five men generally make up a good-sized mob.

MOLL-BUZZER, a pickpocket who robs only women.

MOUTH-PIECE, a thief in the pay of the police.

MUG. This word really means face, but the crook uses it for photograph as well. A mugged thief is one whose picture is in the rogues' gallery.

N

NICK, to make a "touch."

P

PERCENTAGE COP-PERS, policemen and detectives who protect thieves in exchange for a percentage of their plunder.

PETER, a safe.

PETER - MEN, safe - blowers, bank men, etc.

PORCH-CLIMBER, second-story house worker.

PROP - GETTERS, thieves who make a specialty of "lifting" scarf-pins.

Q

QUEER, counterfeit money.

R

RAP, knock, beef, and squeal.

REEF A LEATHER, means raising the lining of a pocket in which the pickpocket has located a "book." It is a difficult undertaking.

S

SHOVER OF THE QUEER, an utterer of counterfeit money.

SLOUGH - WORKER, country-house worker.

SPOT, term in prison. A "one spot" means a sentence of one year.

Glossary

SQUARE IT, to give up grafting.

SQUEAL. In the case of a grafter, to betray another grafter. In the case of a victim, to make a fuss over his loss.

STIR, penitentiary.

STOOL-PIGEON, a thief in the pay of the police.

STRONG-ARM MAN, highwayman.

SWAG, plunder other than cash, such as silks, jewelry, etc.

SWEAT-BOX. A prisoner is put in the sweat-box when he is browbeaten by the police in order to make him divulge secrets in his possession. In New York this is called the " Third Degree."

T

THIMBLE, a watch.

TIP-OFF. A thief considers himself " tipped off " when a mouthpiece or detective points him out in the street or " calls the turn " on him at the Front Office.

TOOL, the man in a " mob " of pickpockets who does the real " nicking," i.e., gets the pocketbook or roll of money.

TOUCH. A man has been " touched " when the " tool " has got his " leather."

Y

YEGG-MEN, tramp thieves. They are to be found largely on the railroads.